Sunup to Sundown

Sunup to Sundown:

Watermen of the Chesapeake

By Mick Blackistone
Photographs by James Parker

ACROPOLIS BOOKS LTD.
WASHINGTON D.C.

In the photograph opposite the title page the Lorraine Rose in
the marsh of Knapps Narrows, Tilghman Island, has seen her last oyster season.

ACROPOLIS BOOKS, LTD.
Alphons J. Hackl, Publisher
Colortone Building, 2400 17th St., N.W.
Washington, D.C. 20009

Attention: Schools and Corporations
ACROPOLIS books are available at quantity discounts with bulk purchase for educational, business, or sales promotional use. For information, please write to: SPECIAL SALES DEPARTMENT, ACROPOLIS BOOKS, LTD., 2400 17th St., N.W., WASHINGTON, D.C. 20009.

Are there Acropolis books you want but cannot find in your local stores?
You can get any Acropolis book title in print. Simply send title and retail price. Be sure to add postage and handling: $2.25 for orders up to $15.00; $3.00 for orders from $15.01 to $30.00; $3.75 for orders from $30.01 to $100.00; $4.50 for orders over $100.00. District of Columbia residents add applicable sales tax. Enclose check or money order only, no cash please, to:
ACROPOLIS BOOKS LTD.
2400 17th St., N.W.
WASHINGTON, D.C. 20009

Library of Congress
Cataloging-in-Publication Data
Blackistone, Mick.
    Sunup to sundown.
    1. Fishing—Chesapeake Bay (Md. and Va.)   2. Fishers—Chesapeake Bay (Md. and Va.)   3. Chesapeake Bay (Md. and Va.)—Social life and customs.   I. Title.
SH464.C47B58 1988   639'.22'0916347
88-24097
ISBN 0-87491-891-X

Book design by Pamela E. Moore

dedication

No matter what time my brother and I got up, dressed, and went down on the wharf, she was already there. She wore a long, shapeless dress, a light sweater, and a sun bonnet of yellow straw. I watched as she propelled her wooden skiff through the marsh with her dipnet. The morning mist rose lazily from the grass where, no doubt, the muskrats watched with equal curiosity. Some mornings she would wade along the shore, her dress wet and flowing behind her, the skiff and crab basket in tow. Her quick reflexes left little chance for crabs hiding in the grass to escape. As I watched her throughout the summer and over the years, she never ceased to amaze me: never speaking, always looking, going along the marsh in a rhythm that made time stand still. She was Miss Dorothy Banigan. She looked to me to be in her 80's and she was my first introduction and seduction to working on the water.

Miss Dorothy has crossed my mind often throughout the last 35 years, regardless of where I have been living or what I have been doing. Perhaps she is the reason for this book, or, perhaps it is the countless stories I heard from my father while growing up. There were stories of black butlers and servants who watched over the Blackistone children to make sure the boys weren't shanghaied by an oystering captain pulling up to the wharf looking for young deckhands for trips up the Potomac to Washington buyers. And tales of oystermen conducting their drinking, swearing, and fighting in my grandfather's bar several hundred yards from the Big House where my father had to "stay put" as a boy because my grandmother would not allow him near "those men." Then there were the many times I went with my father to Joe Bailey's store, Frank Gas's bar, T's-Cove, Capt. Sam's, the Old Gum, or countless other "stopping off" watering holes where he loved to spend hours talking to watermen and farmers about family, friends, oysters, rockfish, crops, Washington politics, and a cornucopia of other subjects, mostly because he loved these "cronies" and partly because it made my aunt, Jane Blackistone Hughes, upset that he spent so much time in one place or another.

These were all fascinating people to me, these men who provide the bounty from the Bay—oysters, clams, fish, crabs—to millions of people day in and day out. These men whose words are carefully chosen, bluntly honest, and used sparingly, and, whose light-hearted remarks come in instantaneous jibes, barbs, and jokes that cut another's jugular so fast he can bleed to death before the others stop laughing. These men who are tough enough on the outside to weather sub-zero oyster dredging expeditions on a daily basis in February and soft enough on the inside that a small child can warm a heart and bring a tear to their eyes. Men who follow the water because it's "what we do" and who see more sunrises in a month than most of us see in a lifetime. Their lifestyles have changed little over the generations, but the world around them is changing quickly. James Parker and I spent over a year with the men looking into their lives on the water. They are facing serious issues of pollution, development, and government regulation. Issues that are having a severe impact on their way of life. Their colleagues in the coastal states from Florida to Maine, California to Washington, and the Great Lakes face the same issues. This book is about them and for them. We hope it will help more of us understand the watermen in perspective of the 80's and get more of us to ask and answer the question, "Where they will be in the future?"

This book is dedicated to men and women who work on the water and to the children of future generations in the hope that they will come to know the values of our national bays and rivers system. A portion of the profits of the sale from *Sunup to Sundown* will be donated to the Maryland Watermen's Association.

table of contents

Chapter 7: Crabbing into Summer......203

preface

While there may be many users of the Chesapeake and its ecosystem, the watermen are the real people of the waters. Whereas others seemingly pass through as recent arrivals, the watermen have been on the Bay for hundreds of years. It is their world and in return for their understanding and appreciation it has supplied them with their needs. They do not have to bulkhead the waterfront to build massive developments, for they know how to work the water, and land, and thus earn a living in countless ways, though often hidden to outsiders. They know the sea grass and where the crabs or fish are lying, when the eels move from the mud and sand to deeper water. They know when the red tides come and areas of the estuary that are "dead waters" because of lack of oxygen. They recognize the weather and seasonal changes that can bring a multitude of changes in growth and migration within hours. They know the sounds and feel of the water and when crabs will shed and fish will move. They know all the secret languages that are denied all outsiders and without which existence on the Chesapeake would be an impossibility.

MSB

acknowledgments

Special thanks and deep appreciation to the following for their tremendous support, advice, input and help on *Sunup to Sundown*.

Larry Simns
Betty Duty
Nancy Mattis
Joe Valliant
John Page Williams
Pati DuVall
Chesapeake Bay Foundation
Citizens Program for the Chesapeake Bay
The Capital Gazette Newspapers
The Baltimore Sun Newspaper
The Dorchester News
Chesapeake Bay Magazine
Maryland Clammers Association
University of Maryland Sea Grant College
Helene Tenner
Maryland Department of Natural Resources
Pete Jensen
Watermens' Gazette
Ronnie Fithian
Bill Lampkins

Robbie Wilson
C.R. Wilson and Crew
Larry Thomas
Gene and Deenie Tyler
Russell Dize
Bill and Jeane Cummings

. . . and countless others who have made this effort possible.

introduction

The Bay

The Chesapeake is America's largest estuary. Of all bodies of water, estuarine systems offer the greatest diversity in water composition. An estuary, according to oceanographer Donald W. Pritchard, is a "semi-enclosed body of water which has free connection with the open sea and within which sea water is measurably diluted by freshwater from land drainage." Within an estuary, freshwater mixes with salt water, each contributing its own variety of chemical and physical characteristics. The mixing of fresh and salt waters creates unique chemical and physical environments, each of which supports different communities of organisms particularly suited to that type of water. The greater number of different environments available within a body of water, the greater the variety of life that is likely to be sustained therein.

The Chesapeake Bay is 200 miles long, with 123 of those miles in Maryland, and from three to 22 miles wide. The water surface of the Bay covers 2,200 square miles. Although the average depth is just 21 feet, it reaches 174 feet off Bloody Point at the southern tip of Kent Island.

More than 2,700 species of plants and animals inhabit the Chesapeake and its shoreline. Forty-six rivers and streams flow into the Chesapeake, some of the principal ones being the Susquehanna, the Elk, the Bush, the Gunpowder, the Sassafras, the Patapsco, the Choptank, the Patuxent, the Honga, the Nanticoke, the Wicomico, the Pocomoke, and the Potomac. Seventeen of Maryland's counties plus Baltimore City border on the Chesapeake, accounting for a total tidal shoreline of 4,100 miles in the State. Its watershed stretches from New York to the Virginia tidewater. There are about 11,000 commercially licensed watermen and women working the waterways.

Like many bodies of water, the Chesapeake has enemies; some old, some new. The Bay's health has been and continues to be threatened by various forms of pollution. Stress on the Bay has been steadily increasing since 1950, as documented in a seven-year Environmental Protection Agency study. Here are some of the problems experienced by the Bay due to pollution, development, and other sources:

- Levels of nutrients, primarily nitrogen and phosphorus, are increasing in many areas of the Bay, especially the upper reaches of almost all the tributaries.
- The amount of Bay water showing dangerously low (or no) dissolved oxygen in the summer is estimated to have increased 15-fold in the last 30 years. Bay creatures and plants need oxygen to live.
- Elevated levels of heavy metals are found in many areas of the Bay in the water and sediments.
- High concentrates of toxic organic compounds have been shown in the bottom sediments of the main Bay.
- Bay grasses have declined throughout the Chesapeake region.
- Oyster reproduction and harvests have dropped in the past ten years.
- Landings of freshwater spawning fish, such as shad, herring, and striped bass have decreased in recent years. Spawning success of these and other species has been poor.

Captain Larry Simms, President of the Maryland Watermen's Association, clam dredging off Annapolis.

Clams move up the conveyor to the quick hands of Larry Simms and Bear. They have a limit of 15 bushels a day.

Miss Norma, a typical Bay built boat, leaves the harbor for crabs on the Chesapeake.

Larry Simms and Bear picking clams off the conveyor.

Patent tong boats off Rockhall, Maryland.

Working a clam dredge on Dawn II on the Choptank.

Tilghman Island, 4:30 a.m.; the fleet sits before the snow storm.

Abandoned but not forgotten. A home on Hooper's Island, Maryland.

ISLANDS IN THE SUN
A Song by Janie Meneely

When I sail away today I'll set my course for South.
With the tide I'll ride the wind up to the river's mouth.
Then down the Bay I'll sail away. Wing on wing I'll run
Until I see ahead of me my islands in the sun.

> Tilghman, Tangier, Smith, Hooper, Deal.
> Steeples in the summer sky,
> Lilies in the field.
> On your shores I'll drop my sails,
> I'll drop my anchor round,
> And let your comfort cover me
> Until the sun goes down.

I feel the wind against my chin, the wheel hard in my hand.
Sails all bellied fat and full, we pull away from land.
We pull away from work-a-day, from freeways and from phones.
Nine-to-five to say alive: it's good to be alone.

> Chorus

I watch the workboats head for home, their catches in their hold.
Silver in the fish they net; the morning sun, their gold.
Hard enough the life they lead, what peace it seems to me.
If I could trade but for a day, I wonder if I'd leave.

> Chorus

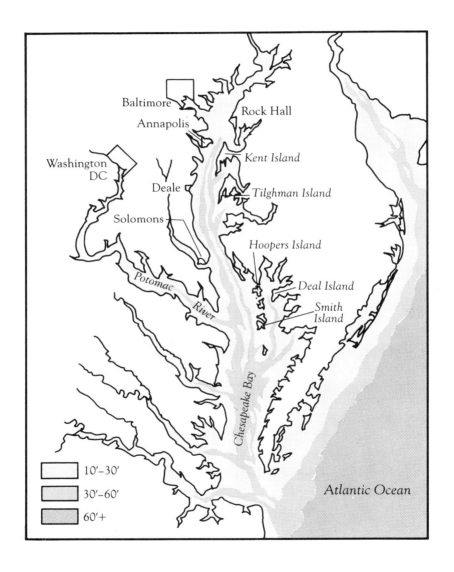

Baltimore

Annapolis

Rock Hall

Washington
DC

Kent Island

Deale

Tilghman Island

Solomons

Hoopers Island

Potomac

River

Deal Island

Smith
Island

Chesapeake Bay

	10'–30'
	30'–60'
	60'+

Atlantic Ocean

"I picked 15 bushels of clams in five hours off the belt, and he (the Captain) can sit in the cabin then come out here and tell me the ones that got by me."

chapter 1

winter clamming

A Day on the Water

At 6:00 a.m. on a cold December morning the phone rang and Larry Simns, Captain of Dawn II, president of the Maryland Watermen's Association, and a waterman all his life answered with a groggy "hello." "Larry, it's Mick, are you going out?" I asked with apprehension and trepidation as the adrenalin far exceeded the caffeine flowing through my veins. "Yea. We got market today. I'll meet you at the Naval Academy parking lot about 6:45; I'm driving a Ford pick-up. You ride with me. Dress warm and wear boots." He hung up. "Wear boots," I thought. "Damn, it's going to be cold and wet." Market meant he had a buyer and that we would be clamming today for his 15-bushel limit and I would have the honor of working with him and his mate. It also meant I would have to dress for a day on the water when the temperature would start out in the low twenties and the wind chill factor would bring it far below zero.

As we reached the dock, morning light was available and I grabbed my slicker, hat, lunch (do they eat lunch?), clipboard, and pencils. There were seven workboats tied up, two with diesels breaking the early silence. Men were gathered on Larry's other clamming boat, DAWN, talking among themselves. All of them came a bit more alive as we approached the DAWN. Alive, first because the Captain was present, and second, because there was a stranger in their midst — me. No one acknowledged my existence. "Put your stuff in the cabin there. We'll take her out," Larry said and I responded. The men spoke sparingly to each other and moved into action, wiping condensation and frost from windows, lighting kerosene heaters in the cabin, checking clam baskets and equipment, and generally making ready. I stood anxious to work, become a part, be accepted; nobody spoke to me. Larry came into the cabin where I sat sheepishly, watching and listening. Within minutes five men were in the cabin: "Bear," "Crow," "Magnum," Larry, and me. Crow runs DAWN. He and Bear were there to get paid. "Magnum," or Tom Lukenich, is Larry's mate on DAWN II. He will go with us today.

"Got market today, I suppose?" Magnum asks out loud, staring through the frosted windshield. "Son of a bitch. We ain't had no market for soft-shell clams and oysters neither. Ain't no oysters hardly anywhere. Lest we can make some money clammin'." He continues speaking through the glass. No one responds. Larry is paying Bear and Crow.

"Where you goin', Bear?" Tom asks.

"Bill's sick, so we ain't goin' out. I'll go over to Cantler's I reckon, less Crow gives me a ride home," Bear responds. "Ain't got much market anyway."

"Hell, wish I was goin' home," Tom responds.

"Too much partying last night, huh Magnum?" Crow interrupts.

"Hell, Larry, he was t'over mixin' screwdrivers an' t'wasn't but half glass orange juice to spread over a whole bottle of vodka."

"Yea, it was," Tom responds sheepishly, as he pulls his hat on. Crow says, "What ya doin' with that hat - heatin' the air between your ears?" "That'll be so," Tom replies.

The jibes start to flow but are cut off quickly with Larry angrily saying "Goddamit, there's too much smoke in here. Put those goddamn cigarettes outta here." Bear moves quickly to the door. Crow extinguishes his in an empty Coke can sitting on the dining table winks at me and puts his in the can after Crow. I think to myse__, __e winked, so at least he knows I'm here.

Crow and Bear leave, Larry cranks up the twin Caterpillar diesels, Magnum moves outside to free the lines, and we're off. Charlie Scott's Marine is next door to the watermen's dock. Charlie is one of Annapolis' top sailors, winning many local, national, and international sailing events over the years. I think for a moment about these men going out on the water doing their work and Charlie going out to do his. Both represent Maryland well, and though from different worlds, are neighbors.

It is a quiet ride out to the clamming bed. Larry and Tom worked the area yesterday. A plastic bleach bottle tied to a line in the water to starboard marked the spot where they would set the conveyor into action. It was cold on deck as we left Mill Creek and headed toward White Hall Bay, a short distance from Annapolis Harbor and the mouth of the Severn River.

The cabin is warm thanks to the kerosene heater that Tom fired up a half-hour earlier. Larry moves silently, turning on the radio, depthfinder, radar, and countless other dials. DAWN II was designed by Larry, and built from the hull up by his friend Phil Jones in Hoopers Island, on Maryland's lower Eastern Shore. She was launched this past summer and is a beautiful piece of work, equipped with bunks, head and shower, oven, microwave, stereo, and more. Unlike most working skiffs that characterize the Chesapeake workboat fleet, she looks more like a yacht than a workboat. At 46 feet long and 18 feet broad, she has a high bow and an unusually large cabin to accommodate potential charter fishing groups from the city to supplement Larry's income. The conveyor for clamming on the starboard, or right side of the boat, runs almost her length. The three-foot-wide mouth that dredges along the bottom is fed by hydraulic lines and a fire hose that crosses the deck amidship between twin engine boxes, pump engine, and lots of iron work. The conveyor hangs onto iron trestles via an intricate arrangement of chains, cables, pulleys, springs, and lines. Along with all other clamming boats, she is the most complex kind of workboat. The clamming rig alone costs about $20,000 and parts must be replaced constantly. DAWN II also has been designed and constructed to allow switching to oyster or crabbing rigs, which add thousands more dollars to an investment that represents a lifetime working on the water and saving patiently. Brand new, her price peaked at more than $175,000.

"Gonna pick some clams today?" Tom asks me.

"I hope I get to," I responded awkwardly. It was the first dialogue we had since I entered his world.

"This is Mick. He's writin 'a book." Larry gave his full and final explanation of my presence.

"A book! Am I going to be in it?" Tom asked with some excitement.

"Hell no," Larry interrupted, "what's he want to write 'bout you for? He's writin' about people who 'work' on the water."

"Shit, I work. Long as I'm aboard, it's the reason you don't have to. Got some clams yesterday, didn't we?"

"Yea, we did, but you let a load slip off the back there."

"I'll be damn, you just sit up here in the cabin then. I'll show you clam pickin'," retorts Tom.

"Bout time, if it was up to you, wouldn't matter the market. I have to show you the clams to make sure you get them right. Goddamn."

"Yea, I will," Tom explained as he began to put on his oilskins and sweatshirt over several layers of flannel and wool.

I realized I had just witnessed what would be the first of many jibes these two men would throw at each other throughout the hours, days, weeks, and months they would clam the Bay. There were only two degrees of conversation between the captain and mate; serious conversation on where the clams were; what kind and size the buyers were looking for; how the market was turning; the weather and jibes, jokes, and sarcasm that broke the monotomy and lifted the cold, lonely, isolated spirits that would mark hours on the water alone. Even in this force of two, there was no democracy. The captain is the man in charge and responsible for all aspects of the entire operation — the crew works for him. There are no questions asked. I would see this pattern on every boat and in each harvest, regardless of their quest. Ronnie Fithian, a Rock Hall waterman said one day, "The Captain may be wrong but he's still the Captain."

Tom exits to set some 20 feet of six-inch-wide fire hose off the port side and then primes the pump to an auxilliary motor. This would send Bay water with tremendous pressure into the water's end of the conveyor belt and rinse mud and sand from the clams, oyster shells and other debris that came up the belt, which ran some 45 feet along the entire starboard side of DAWN II. Tom could raise or lower the clam dredge so that it moved along just under the Bay floor enough to "ride the contours" and pick up clams. Larry positioned the boat to begin, asked Tom if he could hear him through the radio loudspeaker, and set DAWN II on a straight course at about 1 1/2 knots for several hundred yards.

Clams, oyster shells, rocks, and bottles came up the conveyor. Tom, at the stern, leaning over the belt, had three, five-gallon plastic buckets on the gunwale. He would pick the desired clams off the stainless steel belt and put them in the buckets. About two buckets would fill a bushel basket. Fifteen legal baskets would be filled today and three "illegal." There is a sign in the window of the cabin: "Damn—such a deal BUY TEN GET ELEVEN." I would later learn that the buyers want 11 bushels, but will pay for ten. At the going price of only $17 a bushel compared to a good $60 a bushel in times past, this grates on the clammers.

Tom is picking, and I sit uncomfortably in the cabin with Larry, a thousand questions doing cartwheels in my mind. Finally, I ask about working on the water.

"It seems watermen are always losin' nowadays. For every step forward we take two steps back, but the retreat is slower if we're out here workin'."

The Chesapeake Bay area has become increasingly popular as a place to live. Real estate prices in the past decade have sky-rocketed and people are still moving into developments as fast as they can be built. County governments, like Anne Arundel, which borders on the Chesapeake or her tributaries, have established community and economic development offices to court businesses on a national and international level to seek their relocation to the Bay area.

In 1983, in response to growing concern about the environmental integrity of the Chesapeake, the Governors of Maryland, Virginia, and Pennsylvania, and Marion Barry, Mayor of Washington DC, signed the first Chesapeake Bay Agreement which then served as a

catalyst for the Chesapeake Bay Critical Areas Commission and legislation essentially to regulate and monitor development and land use
within 1,000 feet of the Chesapeake Bay. The watermen are very skep-
tical of this legislation and its effect on stopping development. They
know that developers have put in permit applications prior to the Bay
Agreement, which means that regardless of the new regulations, development can and will still take place.

Watermen have three major problems according to Larry Simns:
Population, pollution, and government intervention.

"We can survive the natural cycles, but not the man-made problems
that are added to those cycles. The developers and population growth
in our areas crowd the watermen and their families out. There's less
and less room for us to live and work. And the goddamn bureaucrats
make laws restricting us from making a living in the disguise of
conservation.

"Environmentalists and government workers have time to make the
laws that kill us. Self-employed people don't input to government—
they're too busy workin' the business. It makes it twice as hard for the
waterman because he don't have faith in the government system to
start with.

"The only thing that's important is working for a living and no one
bothering us. Whole damn thing is working—physical work. Ain't got
no prejudice to people red, black, green, or yellow long as they put in a
day's work. Prejudice is against people who don't do physical work.

"Most watermen think the harvest won't go away but population
and pollution—damn if they ain't taken it right fast. Men work over
12 hours a day many a day and then are shocked when they see
changes. A man who works on the water don't see a new house being
built, even the grass changing color, works sunup to sundown too
often, dark to dark, don't read papers for zoning or legislative issues—
hell, he has to worry about tomorrow's market.

"A life of self-destruction's what it is. Watermen are preoccupied
with day-to-day and not working on big problems. And watermen
fight the system and each other too. I swear, we're all crazy
sometimes."

The dimension of waterfront development and its impact on the
seafood packing homes is that the packers can often retire on the pro-

ceeds from the sale of their property. The Maryland Watermen's Association (MWA) reports that 90 percent of the Chesapeake's clams are being processed out of state. The consequences of this are troublesome because when the oysters come back from hard times, few packing houses will be left open to shuck them.

"Maryland's missing the boat," Larry Simns says. "We're sending thousands of jobs out of state when we send the clams out to be processed."

As I sit and listen to his running thoughts, Larry turns to take the DAWN II in a slow arc to retrace the clam bed. Tom takes a moment to light a Marlboro. He will have about 35 seconds of relaxation before the conveyor brings the clams, shells, and debris up to his now numbing fingers. Larry gets a call over the VHF. Crow is checking with Larry to see how their bed is working. He talked to other clammers and picking is moderate.

Larry glances back at Tom and tells Crow we will have limit by 1:00 if things keep up. I soon learn that the radio is on constantly to break the monotony, find out how other men are doing, and to spread a variety of lies about location, quality of picking, and where the other boats are working. There are about 300 clam boats working the Bay. There are only seven within eyesight of DAWN II this morning. Most of the other boats are on the Eastern Shore.

The clam dredge went back to work and Tom's steady picking reassures Larry that he can talk to me some more. I wait silently and impatiently for him to continue.

"It's not the money. It's the way of life. Whether you're born into it or come into it, a real waterman will work the water through good and bad 'cause he loves it out there. We're all damn crazy fools, but it's what we do and ain't one that wants to do 'nother thing. The ones in the money are in the seafood business, not the working waterman."

"I'll tell you it ticks me off to hear people say we're the farmers harvesting the Bay. Hell, we ain't like farmers. Watermen, I line up with the Indians." He proceeds to give me an analogy that brings me to a level of concentration that even leaves the sound of the engines out of mind.

"See, the Indians welcomed the white men with open arms and let them come into their land, and before they knew it the white men cut down on the Indian's territory, took his game and his way of makin' a livin' and changed his way of life. They didn't get too involved with the white men, just let them in, they didn't get involved in government 'cause they didn't understand it or trust it anyhow, and they tried to keep stayin' the same while all this change was goin' on around them. On top of that, the tribes fought with each other and rarely worked together. Hell, the chiefs had a helluva time. Then they all woke up one day with white men down all around them, and no hunting land as government and population swallowed them up. Same thing with the watermen. Development is closing in on our communities. Rich people are buying the farms and don't allow the boys to hunt. The marinas now with recreational boats don't want us in their yards or slips because the boaters complain watermen's work is dirty, messy, and noisy, so there's fewer places for us to go. And the watermen can't pay $40 an hour labor in a yard or $10 a foot to haul a boat out. So we're in a goddamn mess and some don't know it 'cause they're workin' their tails off to keep up everyday."

Moments later I join Tom at the stern to help him pick clams for several hours. The wind is blowing a steady, moderate breeze and it's about 30 degrees, less, of course, the wind chill factor. Tom says to pick the large black clams that he misses. I watch the stainless steel belt bringing the clams forth and I am struck by how quickly he collects three, four, five clams in one hand, places them in one of the five gallon buckets, while his other hand recoils for more. We are wearing a watermen's trademark; thick rubber gloves, wet and cold on the inside, far exceeding the December temperature on the outside. Tom says it's awkward picking with gloves but your hands will get "tore up" if you don't. I decide to keep the gloves on.

After about three hours, my five-gallon bucket is about 3/4 full. Tom has snatched up at least six bushels in this timeframe. Larry joins us at the stern and his right hand instinctively reaches for the boat's rear hydraulic controls to make some minor adjustments in the dredge.

"Ain't ya filled yer bucket yet?" he shouts to me while looking over my shoulder. "Tommy doesn't let that many go by, which doesn't give me much chance," I respond with slight embarrassment.

"There goes one, there goes another," he's pointing at clams having passed Tommy and several going by me. "Goddamn, there goes another one. You wear glasses?"

"I have them on. . .contacts," I respond.

"Well take 'em out then, godammit, you're missing a load over the end there," he exclaims.

My nerves are on edge now as I lose another one back to the Bay, hoping he doesn't see it, which is pure fantasy. Larry returns and goes to the cabin.

"Goddamn, I hate it when he comes back here pointin' and saying there goes one, there goes one'," says Tom. "He does that to me and I want to say 'get your tail back up in the cabin and leave me pick, you son of a b." He laughs for a second.

I told Tom when Larry pointed to the last one I missed, I was ready to jump overboard and find the damn thing. Tom laughed loudly.

"You're pretty new at this stuff so he'll give you another five minutes to get the hang of it." He laughs briefly and returns to silence and picking.

I return to the cabin when we have about reached our quota. My hands and feet are numb and my knees are stiff. The romantic life of the watermen had left my mindset about 30 minutes ago.

Clam buoys mark the beds where men can collect their day's harvest. The clammers must sight an imaginary line between the marks and stay within the boundaries or face stiff penalties in court. Government planes fly overhead occasionally and will take pictures of a clam boat whose captain accidently runs the bow or stern of the boat across the invisible boundary. Captains have been fined over a $1,000 and received points on their commercial licenses for crossing the line by as little as two or three feet. A photograph from a plane of such a violation leaves little to debate in court; the captains rarely win.

Larry leaves the helm to talk to Tom. He can operate the boat from controls at a stern station. Tom is on his last bushel.

With clams being plentiful this winter and the oyster harvest devastated by a disease called MSX, many of the oystermen have turned to clamming. Larry explains that when there are many clams, it's worse for them because they will flood the market with too many people selling and not enough buying. He is concerned about his share of market but also concerned that oystermen like skipjack captain Russell Dize, who is also running clam boats, make enough money to get by, too.

The buyers tell the clammers what kinds of clams they want and where they want them picked—fat, small, black, whatever—"Buyers screw us and each other too, but it's what we work with—beating every damn system every damn day," Larry explains.

In the winter, the watermen can clam until they get their 15-bushel limit. They cannot start until sunup. In the summer, they can only clam until 1:00 pm because there is no refrigeration on board and the clams will die.

At 1:30 p.m., Larry and Tom shut off the hydraulics and raise the conveyor from the water. We have our quota. With the "sculpture" of bridge work and stainless steel belts fastened securely to starboard, Tom hoses down the deck and DAWN II heads for the dock. Larry goes back to the radio and tells Crow we're heading in.

When we tie up, Larry and I will load the bushel baskets on a home-made wheelbarrow designed to take four bushels at a time to the ice-house at the end of the dock. Larry is meticulously instructing me on where to put the first basket on the wheelbarrow. "If you don't put her there, she'll tip over and we'll lose the whole damn thing overboard. We'll do this—Tommy is too damn dumb to get it right." "They're about to start," I say to myself.

"Hell, too," Tom responds. "Make sure you get in your book who done the pickin' and who sat on his ass," he instructs me. Larry smiles.

"Bout time you did some goddamn work. Mick don't want you in his book. Think he's crazy?"

"Yea, he does." I ask Tom for his last name and reassure him of his place in the book.

"Lukenich," he says proudly. I ask him how to spell it.

"Ain't that a helluva damn name," Larry jibes, "Why, he can't even say it much less spell the damn thing. Goddamnist name I ever heard, and its owner ain't worth a damn either."

"Yea he is—picked some clams today didn't we?" Tom seems slightly insecure about the Captain's comment and probably my presence, too. He, like men on other boats I witnessed, will joke with the captain but want to know their work and results were satisfactory. I have witnessed that, to a waterman, hard work is all that matters in the eyes of his colleagues. I reflect too that Larry and the other captains generally take the initiative at terminating brief interludes of jibes and sarcasm and they, more often than not, terminate such sessions with a positive response. They are human, too.

A Little History

The Maryland Watermen's Association was founded in 1973. Larry Simns has been President since that time. Larry was born in Rock Hall, a watermen's town like hundreds of others dotting the shoreline of the Chesapeake and her tributaries. From the time he was eight years old, he knew he wanted to work on the water.

"When I was six years old, I would row a skiff for my great grandfather while he worked a trot line for crabs. When I was 12, I worked out of my own rowboat for soft crabs and running eel pots. I had to crab with my uncle and earn a ride down the Bay to Eastern Neck Island where my boat was. There wasn't any work except on the water for a lot of the men, so when I was 13 I learned to do what they did. Work any job for family support money, but get back to the water because it's your life blood."

At 13 he worked on a farm outside Rock Hall six days a week for $5.00 a week during the summer. When school started he worked for hunters before and after classes. "In the morning I'd put corn and decoys in the field and at night after school I'd go back and bring the decoys in."

During high school he worked in a bakery from 8:00 p.m. to 5:00 a.m., then went to school. "We did anything to make money for the family, but I also wanted to get back on the water, so me and other boys only went to school two or three days a week. If you could land a day's work on a boat you stayed out of school, but we tried to make at least a couple days of school a week. Finally, I got a bigger boat and spent my time crabbing in season. I can tell a young boy who wants to be a real waterman. Hell, he'll work for free just to be on the water."

"Was a time when people used to look up to watermen. Now they don't. Too many families in the community don't work the water and don't want their kids to, either. You have to be good to make it on the water today. You have to hustle to make money," Larry explains.

Dorothy, a woman I chatted with at Tilghman is from Rock Hall and grew up on the water. Like Larry, her perspective is consistent with her "colleagues" around the Bay.

"Girls had two choices: Work in the shirt factory, packing houses or on the water, or marry some fellow who came to town with money and then leave. If you didn't marry someone with money, you couldn't get out and besides, you didn't know what was out there anyway. I tried to encourage all my children to go to college—hopefully away from here—to get away from the water so they could learn there are other things in the world. It's a sad fate to raise your children up and then get them to leave so they don't go through what you did," she says sadly.

"Rather than work in the factory, I worked the water with my husband. I figured if I didn't work with him then, like my mother, I would spend a lot of time alone," she said. This waterman's wife is, like others, defensive of her husband and their lifestyle. "I'd tell the DNR and Washington government types to walk a mile in my shoes. Don't judge and don't hold court until you know all sides. These people don't know the watermen."

Dorothy has left Rock Hall (her husband took off with a younger woman) and has moved to Cambridge to work in a veterinary clinic. She is a woman who, I suppose, reflects each day on her life and her role in the scheme of things. "It's a time when I was growing up you couldn't sleep at night for the racket the swans made in Rock Hall Harbor 30 years ago. None there, now, with development and all. They moved to farms inland. Don't see the geese like you used to. We could dipnet a bushel of crabs in an hour right off the poles. Now there's barely a one on any piling. It's a bleaker life coming with regulations, pollution, and development. It will be tough for many a family to survive. It's true, the watermen don't look at this big picture. I think it's a defense mechanism to look away from sadness and worrying about where everything is heading."

Later Larry explains that most of the captains are married and have to plan constantly for their family, crew, and boat. "We don't figure how much we make in a week's time. We think in terms of a year. What we need to get by and have a little left over. What we don't make on oysters or clams, we have to try to make up with crabs. If that don't work, then take a job here or there to get by. Most of us, at one time or another, have worked on all kinds of jobs. . .boatyard, gas station, tend bar, store, construction; anything to make money enough to get by and hopefully get back on the water in better times. Most return to the water eventually, unless they get so far behind they can't get out."

"The waterman has to constantly adapt to nature's cycles, market, government regulations; with each affecting every product and season different each year. If you don't adjust to changes and innovate by your wits, then it will be tough to make it on the Bay."

"See, problem today in the watermen's community is when they took the fishing away with the moratoriums, the kids lost a lot of work. They used to line up on the piers to unload the boats after school. Now they hang around on corners and smoke dope. There's nothing in town to do except from what they might get from the water. It ain't their fault, it's just a goddamn mess."

Larry has three kids from three marriages. He is separated from his wife now and has been for 12 years. "My daughter is a nurse working on a Ph.D. and is married with two kids. One boy works construction. He would be a helluva waterman, but he makes good money building and I'm glad he's learning a trade. My oldest boy works the water in Rock Hall and takes it one day at a time. I never gave my kids any help financially. If they needed money, they had to learn to work for it. If there wasn't a job around, I'd invent one, but that's the only way to learn."

He is very close to his children and says generically, "Watermen love their families, their boat, their truck, a good drink, and pretty girls." I wonder if there is anything else worth loving. He has worked the water most of his adult life and now is a full-time clammer, sneaking some crabbing in the summer, because it allows him to work near Annapolis where the State House and the Watermen's Association require much of his time during the winter. "I've done this for 15 years. I lose money every year working on the water and running the association." He has tried unsuccessfully several times to turn the job of president over to someone else. There have never been any takers.

"Most days I learn that people only remember what you did that they didn't like and when things work out good on legislation or regulations, everybody wants the credit," he says.

"I can understand politicians even though we don't agree with them. They respond to their constituents and that's who elects them. The constituents don't understand the watermen, so the politicians take stands against us a lot. I try to win some, but lose most. But I can't stand most bureaucrats. They got jobs and can't be fired. They don't care and can't relate to the common working man, so they make decisions that may cost men 25 jobs." Larry's mind is "always working two steps ahead" and he still says "it's one step backward." He averages four hours sleep a night. "I do most of my thinkin' in bed and write notes to myself all night long on a pad by the bed. I try not to spend much time in bed so I don't have to think." I am reminded of Dorothy and her comment of "turning away from sadness."

"A man's got to have a good truck. Almost as important as his boat. Don't do much good to have a boat full of clams and a truck that won't get them to market."

To Market We Go?

On Thursday, December 17, I am scheduled to be at the Maryland Watermen's Association Christmas party. In attendance will be watermen, Department of Natural Resources (DNR) officials, marine trades officials, and members of the press. As at many other watermen's functions, those present will feast on assorted homemade dishes. Betty Duty, administrative assistant to Larry who also runs the MWA on a day-to-day administrative basis, greets us as we enter. Nancy Mattis, who handles membership and insurance for the MWA, greets us as well. There are over 11,000 licensed commercial watermen in Maryland, and the MWA provides the invaluable service of keeping them up-to-date and working for them on harvesting and government regulations, economics, equipment, and more. Larry Simns spends much of his time lobbying the Maryland General Assembly and working with bureaucrats on regulations when he's not working the water. "When I'm in here, I want to be on the water and when I'm on the water, I'm thinking about being in here. It's a helluva mess," he says openly.

Christmas is a special time for watermen. Although Decembers of late have meant oyster diseases, low clam markets, rockfish moratoriums, ice so thick they have tonged oysters through holes cut with saws and axes and other drawbacks, Christmas is when the boats come home and the men spend some time with family and friends.

Though the MWA party ends about 8:00 p.m., there will be many more festivities in the eight days until Christmas. I leave at 6:00 p.m., wish everyone well for the holidays, and arrange to go clamming in the morning. . .if there's a market. "Market" is in the forefront of many conversations; it's the term used to describe the sale of the watermen's products.

Clams thrive in sandy bottoms or where there is a mixture of sand and mud. Submerged aquatic vegetation (SAV) protects natural clam beds from silt, which when allowed to cover young clams in a blanket, kills them. With the gradual disappearance of SAV throughout the Bay over the past 15 years because of pollution and development, many natural beds have been devastated by the dreaded silt. In some areas, clams settle on oyster bars where the oysters protect them from siltation. As the clamming industry grew, an endless harvest of clams in the late 70's often swept clean the natural beds in a matter of months. This situation caused problems because clammers work year round and have tremendous investments in boats and equipment. Some watermen have even had to poach to make the difference be-tween a moderate income and bankruptcy. In the last few years the clamming industry, which at first was a financial boon to many cap-tains, has had its economic tribulations as well.

For several days in early January, clam buyers were still only paying a meager $17 a bushel and with temperatures dropping and ice forming, it was not pleasant by any means. Larry and some of the other clammers, who had market for specified large black clams, decided they would hold up their buyers with a "strike" and tell them it wasn't worth working. The buyers made the unpleasant circumstances more acceptable a day or so later by moving the price to $25 a bushel. By mid-January, the clammers were still at $25 a bushel; the "mini-strike" worked this time.

"We have to do this every once in a while, but the timing has to be right. If they need the clams real bad then they have to have them. You have to play the game and try to get your price when they don't have an alternative. Sometimes it doesn't work, but every once in a while you try," Larry said.

Back in 1987, spring and summer were fairly good seasons for clammers, but prices were still low and supply outweighed demand with buyers paying $18 a bushel in April. In the 1987 strike, the watermen agreed among themselves to stop harvesting for a week; prices rose to $23 a bushel.

The drought that would wreak havoc on Maryland's oyster industry was good for clams, as they need higher salinity to reproduce well and survive. Also, the diseases that kill oysters do not affect clams. Tilghman Island clammer William Roe said the salinity helped pro-duce a good strike of young clams in the Upper Bay, but too much competition drove down the price per bushel.

"What we go through is nothing new," Roe said. "It happens every year." Roe, 53, has been clamming for 34 years. He is past president of the Maryland Clammers Association. "I want them to put a season on clamming. That's what we need," Roe said. He added that for the past three or four years, when harvests have not been as good, clammers settled for $25 to $30 per bushel in the spring when they could have gotten $60 per bushel if they had waited for the peak summer season.

Many Talbot County clammers would like to see a closed spring so they could get more money in the summer, Roe said, but watermen based at Kent Island and those in Rock Hall do not agree.

Roe said clammers are always frantically calling potential buyers in the evenings, trying to find a market for what they will catch the next day. "There's 100 guys fighting for a little bit of clam business," he said. "When you're begging somebody to buy something, you're not going to get much for it."

In August 1987, the clammers faced several other obstacles in their plight characterized by working about half-time for half the catch and half the money they got in 1986. Factors such as local clams being available in New England, with others coming from Canada, over-abundance of clams in Maryland, and more clammers chasing less market all had a serious impact on each individual boat. They were also hit with an embargo ordered by the Massachusetts Health De-partment because northern officials found high bacteria counts in shipments from three Maryland packing houses. Massachusetts im-posed the summer of 1987 embargo on the Warren Denton Seafood Company of Broomes Island, Klas Seafood of Rock Hall, and Rock

Hall Seafood, which provide over one-third of all the clams sold in Massachusetts. The clams were not refrigerated enough during shipping, according to health officials.

With the August embargo in place, the packers had to improve handling putting greater emphasis on refrigeration, and several hundred people, watermen, truck drivers, and shuckers, were temporarily out of work. Maryland health officials had to stress to the public that clams were safe; that the problems were due to handling, not water quality, and that this situation can happen in August when temperatures peak. With September's cooler temperatures, the issue of bacteria counts cools down, too. In order for the embargo on specific packers to be lifted, they had to ship three consecutive loads without a bacteria problem. The embargo proved to be temporary, with little economic threat to most clammers. But, as Ronnie Fithian, President of the Kent County Watermen's Association said, they are always concerned that such embargoes could be ongoing and have broader consequences if not resolved quickly.

"Why workin' sunup to sunset, I looked around one day and asked my wife when we got new neighbors 'cause there were two brand new houses up. She said during oystering when I needed to find my way out of the house and a light to find my way back. Believe it's so, I told her."

Sunrise to Sunset

I called Larry shortly after 6:00 a.m. and there was "some market." Christmas Eve is tomorrow, so Larry plans to get eight bushels of big black clams for the buyer and six bushels of small white clams for Jimmy Cantler, a waterman who owns Cantler's Riverside Inn, a seafood restaurant outside of Annapolis.

As we approach the dock, Larry comments that MSX, the dreaded parasitic oyster disease, has destroyed much of the harvest in Maryland and boats from as far south as Smith Island are entering Annapolis to work oyster beds from around the Bay Bridge and north. MSX has been visible in the past, but in 1987–88 it will prove to be devastating to the oysters in the Bay.

The conversation stops as Larry listens to the diesels of an oyster-tonging boat turn over two docks away.

"Shut her off!" he yells at the man on board. "Shut her off. Goddamn, she sprung a bearing."

"Think so," comes the reply across the water.

"That a Caterpillar?"

"Yea."

"Shut her off now. You'll tear her up good. Hear that squeaky noise? That'a a bearing." Conversation ended. A wave from the other boat confirms it. Two things are certain: Watermen are always in competition with each other for product and looking out for each other's welfare at the same time.

"One thing about engines and women. Every waterman is an expert and everyone has an opinion," Larry explains.

The temperatures had dropped down to the 20's during the night; a sheet of ice coats the deck. "Watch your step, she's a slippery son-of-a-bitch this mornin'." Tom comes up from below. "Where you been?" he quips. "Bout time you got here, we could have been done by now if you was on time. Goddamn, Mick, I have to watch him all the goddamn time," the mate says, feeling confident that Larry will be in a good mood two days before Christmas.

Tom enters the cabin as we head out Mill Creek to the clam bed off the David Taylor Naval Research Center in Annapolis. Tom is excited and pleads with Larry to allow him to place the dredge this morning. He clammed the area with Crow yesterday and found a spot "hotter 'n hell in the summer." In anticipation and hope, his eyes search the horizon for his landmarks and again he pleads, cautiously, with the Captain. Larry remains silent.

"Just this once put her where I tell ya."

"All right. You find your mark?" Larry is sympathetic. I pray that Tom hits a good bed because he has convinced Larry to go with him on this one.

"Head her on out there. See the bleach bottle in the water just to port? We'll run her there."

"Where's the other marks? Goddamn better be able to set me on the other marks if this spot is so goddamn good. Man can't even tell me the marks," Larry jibes.

"Say it's so," Tom says, still excited. "Put her right up there. We'll get some clams today."

Before reaching the clam bed I notice several sticks coming out of the water, one to our port side and one 35 yards to starboard. Larry tells me the sticks form a boundary around leased bottom land and that no one can clam or oyster in the area. It's a serious violation of the law if you get caught working privately leased bottom land. This particular area is leased to watermen, but many are private leases issued by the state for up to 20 years. It will be an issue Larry will soon work on with the Maryland General Assembly because such privately leased bottom and is another example of the "watermen losing their territory", Larry says. I think of the Indians.

The watermen are opposed to this leasing concept because it cuts off their ability to harvest where there is product and "the goddamn bureaucrats are interfering with private lives. Where's the boys from Smith Island going to go to harvest when there's no product down there. He can't come up here if it's all leased. The seafood processing companies with money lease a lot and there's nothing we can do," Larry explains. Leased bottomland and the issue of aquaculture will come up often in the coming months.

I move outside looking for the rubber gloves to help Tom. I make small talk about getting some clams for market and Cantler today.

"No arsters, and no market for clams. Son of a bitch. Ain't no market lately and damn, the clams aren't for holiday tables." He wants to earn wages this close to Christmas.

It's only 11:00 a.m. by the time we have our clams for market and several bushels for Jimmy Cantler's restaurant. After raising, rinsing, and locking into place the conveyor belt, we head for the gas dock to fuel up and unload Cantler's clams. We arrive at about 11:30 a.m. As Tom ties DAWN II up, Larry prepares to fuel her up with diesel. Spotting Jimmy's barmaid down the dock below the restaurant, Larry yells, "Hey, Linda!"

"Hey, Larry."

"Watcha' doin'?"

"Looking for crabs," she explains walking into a storage building.

"Can't find any crabs around here. Have to go to Baltimore to get crabs!"

"Hush up. Not that kind of crabs!" she laughs and goes back up-stairs to the bar.

Jimmy Cantler comes down the dock. He and his family have worked the water all their lives, but now his Riverside Inn requires full-time attention. I have known Jimmy Cantler by reputation for some time and have been to lunches at the restaurant where Maryland's Governor William Donald Schaefer has been lobbied by Larry and his colleagues. Jimmy doesn't acknowledge me, however, and goes imme-diately to inspect the clams Tom has placed on the dock. Tom is still ecstatic over the catch today from his "chosen" spot.

"Ain't they pretty, Jimmy? Goddamn, them's some pretty clams. Prettiest clams I seen in a long time."

Jimmy says little and breaks a clam open. "Fat, meaty girls aren't they?"

"Prettiest clams I set eyes on," Tom continues.

"Jimmy, you know Mick Blackistone?" Larry interrupts.

"Yes. We met about 40 years ago a time or two. And it's Black-i-stone, not Blackstone. Say the 'i'. Goddamn, Larry, that's how you say his name. I make a point of knowing all this shit, ya see. Keep up with the important stuff." Jimmy looks at me. "How ya doin' Mick? They need an extra hand today?" Larry interrupts to tell him that I'm writ-ing a book about watermen and have been crewing and going out with a lot of the men. Jimmy shrugs. Apparently, the book is of no conse-quence to him. I feel dejected for a second. I wanted to spend a lot of time with Jimmy Cantler, but he only ignored reference to the project. He heads up the dock with the clams in his wheelbarrow. About 25 feet away he stops by the diesel pump and turns around. "Come see me after the first of the year, we'll talk," he says and with a motion he's moving up the dock, with no other words necessary.

I am constantly amazed by the watermen's perceptiveness about the world and people around them. Nothing, not even a subconscious fa-cial expression like the one I must have made when I thought Jimmy Cantler was rejecting me, seems to slip by them. I will be reminded often of their perception in the many months ahead.

With the fuel tank topped off, we cast off for Mill Creek and the dock. Larry calls Crow on the radio and finds that he is already at port. Larry asks if we got clams for Bill, who was sick again today, and if he stacked them in the truck to take to the Rock Hall, Maryland buyer, an hour-and-a-half ride from Annapolis. Crow confirms and the radio is silent. Larry explains that Bill got the flu so he agreed to get clams for him. It would allow the crew to make Christmas money and help Bill at the same time. "If we don't help each other from time to time, who will?" he asks.

At the dock, Tom is anxious to get paid and get off. He stays with an aunt, who lives next to the boatyard, during the week and with his girl-friend on Kent Island on weekends or when he's off. "You can't find the crew anytime. They get money on Thursday, drink and party and come to me for a loan on Monday," Larry says. "I have them call me every morning to see about market 'cause I don't know where the hell they are the night before." Crow comes down from Rock Hall every day. That's a trip, but he stays with his mother there. . .I think." Larry says he wants to change the oil in one of the engines. Tom frowns, knowing he's stuck until the Captain says he isn't!

With the engine cover off, Larry must drain the oil from the pan quickly before the chill thickens it up. He has a new suction pump and inserts one tube into the engine block and the other into a five-gallon can for used oil. He places two clamps to the boat's battery to give the small oil pump motor some juice and waits for the old oil to be si-phoned up. The oil must be changed every 200 hours or so. The si-phoning pump doesn't work. He plays with it for a few minutes as Tom and I watch anxiously. We are soon joined by Crow and George.

"What's the matter?" Crow asks as he climbs aboard DAWN II.

"Son-of-a-bitch don't work. Goddamnit. . .ain't this a fine piece of shit. Use it one time and the son-of-a-bitch don't work. Take a look at her Crow. Son-of-a-bitch." Larry is impatient and angry.

"I don't know why you buy this new-fangled shit. The props on the pump motor is shot. See them torn up," Crow responds.

"Goddamn, I only used her once, for Chrissake."

"Don't matter. That's all you're going to use her, too."

"Well, we got to get that oil out with the old hand pump and change the filter. Need to tighten the bolts under the pan, too."

Crow moves to take over the operation without being told. He has worked with Larry long enough to know he doesn't need instructions.

"I can't reach those bolts way under there," Crow claims as he lays parallel to the engine, stretching under the block.

"Well, goddamnit, you got the longest arms of anybody standing on the creek, so if you can't reach them I sure as hell can't," says Larry.

"Hold on," Crow claims and calls out for a ratchet with an extension.

"Hey Larry, why don't you send me to mechanic's school so I can make some decent mechanic's wages? It's half of what I do anyway on these goddamn boats."

Larry is silent to Crow's jibes. He is in no mood to joke around. The oil must be changed and the temperature is dropping.

An hour later, new oil is in engine number two and Crow heads for his truck. He will take 15 bushels of clams to the Rock Hall buyers, over an hour away, unload, and drive back to Annapolis late in the evening. There is no discussion about the fact that it will be another 13- or 14-hour day by the time it's over.

Larry has a bad back, so his efforts are limited in terms of certain lifting and movement. He pushes the wheelbarrow with four bushels of clams aboard down the 125-foot dock and up a 20-foot ramp to the ice house for storage. I will help him stack the clams. He trusts me to do that but not to push the loaded wheelbarrow; "I don't want you to risk spillin' the son-of-a-bitch."

Tom is sitting on the dock still waiting for word of leave. I notice from the protrusion at the back of his shirt that he is wearing a back brace. I would later learn that five years oystering "tore up" his back and knees. "That's hard friggin' work and it'll send your body to a grave 'fore your mind knows where it went," he says.

A Winter Break

The scenes with Larry, Crow, Tom, and others during winter days of December and January would be repeated without me. I would leave them to work with the oystermen aboard skipjacks and tonging boats. I realize that with the exception of changes in nature's way, there is little difference in the men or their methods from one boat to the next.

The men are in harmony with their work today just as their fathers and grandfathers before them. I will return to clam with them in the spring and summer and I am confident that when I return, I won't have missed a beat. They will be performing the same work, in the same way and still hoping for market. They will still be amazed that people in New England want 95 percent of their clam catch to steam, fry, or put in chowder, because to watermen a clam is something they used for bait or chum in years past, "I never thought there was a man alive who would eat one of them things," Tom says.

Let the Politics Begin

The next day it's raining and there are gale force winds on the Bay. There will be no clamming. The men will go out in rain, snow, hot weather or cold 12 months a year, but Larry doesn't want to play with this wind and there is no market anyway. He has other issues on his mind.

About three that afternoon, I'm in the Maryland Watermen's Association office. Larry and Betty are telling me that the Department of Natural Resources wants to collect a five percent excise tax on all commercially documented workboats. This will be the first time they have ever been hit with a five percent tax on the value of their vessels and the DNR wants to include them in the 1986 Boat Excise Tax originally aimed at out-of-state recreational boaters who keep their boats in Maryland and never pay sales, use, or title taxes to the state. The Department wants to collect taxes back to 1976 and the watermen throughout the state are calling the Association to ask for advice.

"I tell them not to pay anything 'til we can figure what to do," Larry explains. "These boys can't afford a five percent tax. Commercial boats should be exempt, like always. They're tying us into that goddamn excise tax law."

Larry knows that I am working on a bill for the General Assembly to allow reciprocity for out-of-state boaters who have paid sales tax in their home state to get credit in Maryland. I sense he is asking for my help, without really asking. I tell him and Betty to give me a copy of the DNR memo and that I will talk to Delegate John Astle, Chairman of the Anne Arundel County Delegation, who is drafting a bill for the Marine Trades Association of Maryland and see if we can't get him to add an amendment that would exclude commercially documented workboats, or at least exclude all boats commissioned prior to the passage of the law in July, 1986. Larry ends simply with "See what you can do for us." Betty walks me to the door and whispers, "Thanks a lot, we really appreciate this. It will kill our men if they have to pay it."

Walking down Maryland Avenue's cobblestone streets toward the State House, I am both upset and pleased. Upset that this kind of lobbying and legislative work will keep me from joining the men on the water for some time and pleased that Larry "asked" for any assistance I can provide.

The Wednesday after Christmas is the Commodore's Eggnog Party at the Annapolis Yacht Club. I will attend the black-tie affair and I plan to grab Delegates John Astle and Elizabeth Smith, who serve in the Anne Arundel Delegation. Smith is also a ranking minority member of the House Ways and Means Committee, which will hear the excise tax bill during the General Assembly session in January. I'm hoping they will push for an amendment or additional legislation to exclude the watermen from the excise tax to solve the problem. A commitment is all I need for Larry at this point. The real battle will take place during the hearings. I feel remotely optimistic, since Betty and John are friends of the marine industry, both commercial and recreational. As it turns out, they both agree at the party to work with us. "No promises, but tell Larry we'll talk after the holidays. And you get with Remi Waley, my legislative aide, to work out the details. Be prepared to address the delegation first about the 14th of January," Astle said. Phase One completed. I want to tell Larry and get back out on the water.

Preparing the jib sail for a day of racing with the wind.

Skipjacks becalmed off Annapolis during a race.

Culling on the Choptank River while watching for the dredge to deliver more oysters and debris to the deck.

Waiting for the dredge to bring another 250 lb. load of oysters to the deck. Then the culling starts.

Jerome and Stevie working a dredge on the skipjack Elsworth.

Culling oysters on the skipjack Elsworth.

"Captain" C.R. Wilson, 13, aboard his boat Tuff e Nuff has hand on the steering stick and a dip net in the other to scoop crabs off his mile-long trotline.

Grabbing the steel rings on the dredge helps William (left) lift the load and dump it on deck.

"Never could figure what goes first. . . year back, knees or brains. I told a boy from Tilghman Island must be the knees or back, no waterman has brains haulin' oysters with a gale blowin' up his ass."

chapter 2

oystering on the bay

Tilghman Island

On October 24, 1987, James—my photographer for the book—and I went to the Annual Tilghman Island Day Celebration. This was a time for the Eastern Shore's island inhabitants to open their doors to the world on a day for recognizing the watermen and celebrating the start of a new oyster season. There was seafood for sale everywhere. . . We immediately went to the Tilghman Island Volunteer Firehouse. The oysters were fantastic, the conversation friendly, and the money raised would purchase new fire equipment.

As we walked through the streetside displays and crowds, I noticed James in serious thought as he fiddled with his camera. "You, okay?" I asked. "Yea, fine," he said. That was about the extent of most of his conversations when he was working.

James is serious about this project. He has been working with me on the concept since the very beginning and is committed to make the right statement about the watermen through his photographs. He is fascinated by their way of life, their philosophy about work, and their conflicts with government and outsiders. I always sense that James, like me, loves being around these men and women, and that he wants to be accepted by them. With his longish hair and wire-rimmed glasses, wearing his ever-present baseball cap and blue jeans, he is often inconspicuous as he moves in deathly silence, madly clicking away.

At 34, he is running his photography studio in Baltimore, working on several houses he has under construction in Annapolis, and shooting pictures for this book. He is a workaholic and, at times, he is so within himself that we don't speak for hours. I'm always confident, however, that he is acutely aware of my feelings for what I would like him to capture on film. We work well together and for that I am most thankful.

Tilghman Island Day greets the oyster season each year and attracts thousands of visitors to the tiny community across the Knapps Narrows Bridge about 20 minutes south of St. Michael's. The tourists come for a glimpse of the watermen and their way of life and the "show" they receive is worth the price of admission:

> Workboat docking contests
> Crabpot pulling contests
> Workboat class and open races
> Skipjack races
> Tours of oyster packing houses
> Exhibits and crafts prepared by
>   watermen and their families
> Music, food, and friendship in the
>   good old fashioned way.

Tilghman Island is a town that lives and breathes the Chesapeake. Founded in 1659, most of its men work in some capacity related to the water. The women and children do likewise. The Chesapeake has provided for them and destroyed them over generations and the inhabitants will take every opportunity to thank and "cuss" this great body of water.

Shirley, the friendly manager of Garvin's Nothing New Shop on Main Street, was having a wonderful time on Tilghman Island Day 1987. Everyone on the island had forgotten their worries for one day and the community was "makin' some money and givin' outsiders a glimpse of what we do down here."

"What you see out there behind the house is a beautiful piece of God's work," she said. "Our men know it and work it same as their fathers before them. They don't ask for much, it's all most of them know. But times are different now than they were 30 or 40 years ago. It's hard and the younger watermen worry a lot about their families and making a living. Why a waterman in his 20's or 30's from down here knows more about the water and how to work it than most people know about their jobs at retirement. They have to learn it early, because as beautiful as the Chesapeake is, she can destroy you with her temper or by taking away your harvest in a heartbeat. These boys know that and it worries them. Same as it does the fellows on Smith Island, Tangier Island, Deal Island, or Rock Hall. You can't show me a waterman who isn't worried some today. I was glad and very sad when my son went into service. I prayed he wouldn't work the water even though it has provided for most on the Island. But things are different today, and we all worry for our young people."

We left the store and wandered over to the contests. This is a time for relaxation, fun, competition, and demonstration of abilities. Hundreds of spectators lined the harbor to catch a glimpse of the men preparing for the docking contest. The timed event features the boat operator backing his work boat into a boat slip and tying it up. I was impressed with the ability of the men to reverse workboats, up to 45 feet long, with good throttle, between pilings that allowed less than a foot of clearance on either side and then tie up—all in less than half a minute. C.R. Wilson, a 13-year old, maneuvered his boat into second place ahead of all the adult watermen. Robbie Wilson, C.R.'s father, laughingly exclaimed to the crowd, "I taught him only enough to take second." He beat C.R.'s time by only two seconds.

From the boat-docking contest, the spectators moved like an army of ants through town and out the causeway to the little island. It was, in days past, the home of the local seafood packing house and restaurant, now lost to fire and hard economic markets. From the island we would watch the crab pot-pulling contest and the workboat races both of which took place offshore in the Choptank River.

The crab pot-pulling contest was a new event thought up by a couple of local watermen. At the start of the gun, each boat would set a straight course of ten crab pots attached to a line and float. The boat then would circle and pull the crab pots up with a boat hook as quickly as possible. The fastest time for the several hundred-yard course would be the winner.

The speed races were broken down with competition between length of work boats. Some of the boats in this event were clearly "souped up" for competition and they were the easy winners with their speeds impressive to the crowd ashore.

Tilghman Island Day is a big event on the Chesapeake Bay. It's followed by Chesapeake Appreciation Days, October 31 through November 1, at Sandy Point State Park outside of Annapolis, and the actual beginning of the oyster season. The skipjack captains take the weekend off to compete in the famous Chesapeake Appreciation Days Skipjack Races. According to Captain Gene Taylor of the MARTHA LEWIS, "It's fun, okay, but I do it because maybe by participating, it will help us watermen." I have my doubts about his optimism because in my eyes, Chesapeake Appreciation Days has become a huge commercial extravaganza and the watermen have been lost in the shadows of Bay environmental awareness and commercialism. That's growth and progress I am told by a event's coordinator. James will be aboard the KATHRYN with Captain Russell Dize to take pictures of the race, while I am off to cook clam chowder from 8:30 a.m. until 3:30 p.m. at the Maryland Watermen's Association tent. The Association will use this day to raise money for their coffers.

Betty Duty is an incredible recruiter and I am sure that one of the reasons she is in charge of the concession is that volunteers cannot say 'no' to her. I couldn't, and that's why I'm cooking chowder and James is on the skipjack!

Oyster season started with the hand and patent tongers October 1st, (two weeks later than the normal September 15th start date, to give this year's crop an opportunity to grow a month and a half before the skipjacks set out with their dredging nets). The tongers are allowed by law to take 30 bushels per boat, or ten bushels per man (up to three men), and can work the rivers, inlets, and shoal areas. The skipjacks have a 150 bushel a day limit and can only dredge in the Bay or open water. There is the usual excitement about the start of the season, but an undercurrent of extreme pessimism is present in every man and woman whose livelihood is made on the water. They are coming off a great year for crabs and aware of the devastating enemy about to hit them square between the eyes. . . MSX and the companion disease, Dermo.

"Happiest day of my life was when my son told me he was joinin' the Coast Guard. He would get out and off the ways of the water. I prayed days on end he would do that or college. The Bay has taken a lot of good men down and it's gettin' worse every year now. It's a sad day too, because I'll miss that boy terribly."

Through Kent Island

When you cross the Chesapeake Bay Bridge from the western shore and Annapolis heading east through Kent Island and Kent Narrows on Rt. 50, you eventually leave the new strip of shopping malls and condominium developments that cover this once-rural Eastern Shore area. Kent Island, following what happened to Annapolis, is now a bedroom community to Washington and Baltimore commuters, and the new condominiums start at over $180,000, with a water view.

One waterman from the Island told me he heard about a wealthy man who had a beautiful home built on a point near Eastern Bay. After the man moved in, he realized the watermen started their diesels, with out-of-the-water exhausts, at first light to be on the water at sunup. The noise constantly woke him up so he went to the government authorities to have legislation created restricting watermen from going out on the water so early in the morning—it would be okay after 9:00 or 10:00 a.m. because he would be awake by then. I would hear of many more such stories in the months ahead.

Heading south on Route 50 and taking Route 33 through St. Michaels, the yuppie heartbeat of the Eastern Shore where the town policeman has a Volvo for a patrol car, there are more and more bumper stickers reading, "Quit Beefing—Eat Seafood" and "Don't Be A Crab Or A Waterman Will Get Ya." Tilghman Island is about 20 minutes south of St. Michaels. Pickup trucks begin to take the place of BMW's and Volvos on the deserted roadways.

Tilghman Island measures some three-and-a-half miles from north to south and it's less than a mile wide. Farm land and houses are scat-

tered in the southern portion of the island down to Black Walnut
Point. Modest frame houses dot the northern tip of the island. The
population has remained steady at about 1,500 since the turn of the
century. Here the famed Chesapeake Bay skipjacks are called "drudge
boats" in Eastern Shore dialect for the process of dredging. Most of
the men work on the water.

James and I will stay at Sinclair House, a bed and breakfast owned
and operated by Miss Deenie and Captain Gene Tyler of the skipjack
MARTHA LEWIS. The four bedrooms with one bath are cheerful
and immaculate. The walls are adorned with skipjack prints and
wooden plaques of races Captain Tyler has won with the MARTHA
LEWIS. There are wooden models of skipjacks and one model of four
of the boats is a wind sculpture made by Miss Deenie's father. Miss
Deenie said she and Gene are "both from Smith Island. We left about
33 years ago. His parents and mine—they all worked on the water. We
lived in North Tilghman for over 25 years in a house we built. The reason we bought this place is because the oyster business is terrible.
There really are none and the ones they find are small and it will take
three years for them to grow. MSX is a problem, but the biggest one is
the water is so salty from not having enough rain."

It's the Sunday after New Year's Day and Tilghman is quiet. Gene
Tyler has taken the MARTHA LEWIS across the Bay to Solomons to
try and do better with his catch than the men are doing on the Choptank River. The weather forecast calls for snow and the skipjacks are
only going out on Mondays and Tuesdays, "push days" when the skipjack Captains are permitted to dredge for oysters with the aid of a
small powerboat called a yawl. The yawl pushes the skipjack throughout the day's work rather than dredging under the power of sail. It's
easier and much more efficient. Captain Tyler was playing his odds
that the snowstorm, coming out of the south, would bypass Solomons
and hit the northern Bay hardest. He played his hunch right this time.
In a game of many chances, it takes risks to try and win. Solomons got
less than an inch of snow, but from Tilghman north, the Bay area
would be blanketed with two to four inches and hit with heavy winds.

The Tylers have two sons; Troy is 26 and works with Gene on the
MARTHA LEWIS. Gibbie is 25 and tongs for oysters on his workboat
CASENOVA, with a friend. "Neither of the boys wants a drudge boat.
They want power. They don't want sail. I think before the next ten

years is out drudging will be gone," Miss Deenie says. Gibbie is working to help support his wife-to-be and her six-year-old daughter. Miss
Deenie says, "He has to go out tongin' every day. When the weather's a
blowin', the tongers go up the creek to hide from it."

"With the bills he has and the life he's chosen, he hasn't any choice
but to work every day. It's hard but what else can he do. I knew when
he and his brother were little, they would be watermen and good
watermen too. But now the drudgin's all but gone and I worry about
them a lot. Crabbin' was good this year, but now it's a long day to make
a dollar. Gibbie went tongin' yesterday and it was a good day. He came
back wet to the thighs, wading for them and the three boys got 13
bushels. He could have sold them to Harrison for $15 a bushel, but
chose to load them in the truck and take them to a buyer in St.
Michaels for $20 a bushel. So, the truck's important, but he's still got
to make payments."

Miss Deenie tells me that she worries about the future because very
few watermen have retirement plans other then Social Security and
the government will probably take that away "before we can use it."
Captain Gene Tyler is 58 years old and they want to plan for the future. The Sinclair House, her bed and breakfast, was part of a watermen's wife's plan and eye for that future. "Tourism has taken over St.
Michaels, so we figured it would come here next. I've done it for a year
now and it's done pretty good. When I think that Gene quits drudging
March 15th and we don't see a dollar come in until May, sometimes
June, we need to plan. But, I worry about the kids. The women most
always manage the dollars and do the planning. The men get all that
money, several thousand dollars for a good week drudging, and it will
get away from them. Most of the women have to control it, but the
young people today can't manage money. They make a lot workin' a
good harvest at the beginning of the season, spend over their heads
with credit, and then when there's no market, they can't keep up and
are in real trouble. And they don't want to do anything else but be
watermen. Doesn't do any good to talk to them. It's the freedom and
independence that is in 'em. It's workin' on the water. But it scares me
thinking about my children's future because they only think about the
instant money for a hard day's work."

Her brother, Captain Russell Dize of the skipjack KATHERINE,
would not allow his son on the boat to make money. She says Russell

kept his son from the instant financial gratification so that he couldn't get enticed by false financial rewards. "I thought Russell might raise a sissy because he didn't let the boy work on the water. I wish I had done that many days because his boy is honor roll in the gifted and talented program at the high school and will get out by going to college. He's a real fine boy and Russell had a lot of thought in that hard decision while the boy was coming up. Most of these other boys will work on the water and some will make it if they work real hard. But what else are they going to do. If you put these boys in the city, wouldn't you have a time!"

The concern in Deenie Tyler is a concern that I can only begin to appreciate after months of talking with the watermen and their families. Concern in not being able to predict the future and the fate of the way of life they have known for generations. Concern that if the market for oysters and other products fall off, her children will be at a dead-end in their mid-twenties without a steady income and unable to afford a house on the Island because real estate prices, driven up by wealthy people willing to pay exhorbitant prices for waterfront property, will force them away. Sadness because her way of life is changing too, and there is little she can do about it. "When I lived on North Tilghman and had a waterview, I could see when my husband brought the MARTHA LEWIS home and could fix dinner. I could watch the dock and know if my son was out and when he came in. When we bought this place (Sinclair House) to have another income, I felt totally lost. I didn't know what my family was doing on the water. I didn't think a waterview meant much, but now I sure realize what it means to people buying and selling real estate," she says.

The snow is coming down. I am to call Captain Robbie Wilson of the skipjack ELSWORTH. If she goes out in the morning, I will meet Robbie at 5:00 a.m. at her berth on Knapps Narrows. "Make your call," Mrs. Tyler says, "Those boys go out about everyday unless there's ice or a gale. A little rain or snow won't stop them." I go up to bed with the assurance that Miss Deenie will wake us at 4:00 a.m.

A Bit of Background

In 1988 Maryland's oyster harvest is the worst it has been in 50 years for the watermen and their families. More than 90 percent of the oys-

ter beds have been killed by parasites, Dermo, and MSX. Further, con-
sumer appetites have been weakened because of a media blitz about
MSX that led people to believe they may get sick if they ate affected
oysters. That is not the case, but rumors caused restaurants, caterers,
and individual customers to stop buying. Higher than average salinity
levels, caused by lack of rain in 1987, helped spread the disease.

"At the beginning of the season we could get $26 a bushel and it was
worth leaving home on Sunday at midnight, pushing up the Bay to
Tolchester, working from sunup to sundown and coming home Tuesday night. Now, at $18 a bushel, it ain't worth it. At the beginning of
the season, the captain would be at the helm 36 out of 40 hours at a
two-day stretch. It's hell, but it's worth the money," Robbie says.

With the price and catch down, fewer boats are going out. In October 1987, there were 500 boats working the oyster beds statewide. By
January 1, 1988, there were fewer than 350 boats oystering by dredge,
tonging, or diving. For the first time in 50 years, the Chesapeake Bay
has yielded less than 1 million bushels of oysters. It is expected to yield
less than 400,000 bushels by March 30. "After Christmas, the season
will only last on paper for these men," said William Outten, shellfish
program director for the Maryland Department of Natural Resources
as he explained they may catch enough to make expenses but that is
about all. For the first time in sixty years, Claude Evans, 77, of
Crisfield, missed an oyster season. He captained the LORRAINE
ROSE, but not this year. "I've seen 'em scarce and I've seen a mess of
'em," he said. "I reckon it's as bad now as it's ever been."

"Aside from a lack of funds from dredging, the cost of maintenance
and insurance is prohibitive. With the Pride of Baltimore sinking, the
insurance carriers cancelled all skipjack insurance, so I worry about
the men and the boat goin' down," Robbie explains.

But watermen are eternal optimists. While boats carry 'For Sale'
signs, men are not going out and holding off on expensive repairs.
They all seem to have faith in two things—time and nature returning
to a good cycle. Robbie tells me that five years ago a crewman could
make $1,000 a week at the start of the season. Now it's down to $260 a
week. "Nature played this dirty trick on us. We had a good season
started, but the lack of rain did us in, that and more and more pollution. Skipjack captains have seen MSX for years, so I'll tell you what's
hurt this Bay the most of anything was old Hurricane Agnes. Hurt us

worse than MSX or anything. She started the quick decline and then with all the chemicals and nitrogen and all coming into the water and getting to shallower and shallower ground, we're having to lay seed oysters in shoal areas," Robbie says.

"When they cut out fishing, everybody went to oysters and clams. That's too many and there isn't enough to go around." He pauses for a moment to get the push boat to her full push speed of 6 to 8 knots. "I love the water and I love working on the water no matter what the problems are. I was 12 years old when I got a boat and started working for myself. After being your own boss that long, do you think I'm going to go work for somebody else? Hell, no!"

If watermen are upset about the natural cycles of 1987 to 1988, they are also upset with the government bureaucracy that controls and regulates the oystering industry.

"The government people tell us where they want us to plant oyster seed in March. They say they're doing us all a favor putting out $1 million worth of seed. Hell, if they want to bring oysters back, give the watermen $10 million worth of seed over four years, let us plant it, and tell them where we'd put it. Hell, $1 million ain't shit!"

"The state collects an oyster tax, fifty cents a bushel, then uses the money to pay us to seed in the spring. People think the government is giving us something, but it was our money to begin with. At fifty cents a bushel, if we catch 700,000 bushels, that's no money to work with."

"Let me tell you, we don't always agree with where the DNR wants us to seed, but they give the orders. Why, we have seed beds that haven't been worked for seven or eight years now. They're all silted over and the seed spat won't cling to anything dirty. Now you take the shells we drudge up today, clean as a whistle. DNR should let us back drudge those old beds to loosen 'em up from the silt. But, no, they think they know more than the watermen. We're workin' with them to drudge those old beds."

Ironically, in the early spring of 1988, someone in government must have been paying attention to Robbie Wilson and others. Working in cooperation with approximately 120 watermen, they conducted an extensive bagless dredging program aimed at cleaning up once-productive oyster bars and making them more receptive to spatfall.

As Wilson mentioned, the bars, located primarily in the Choptank

River and Pocomoke Sound areas, are known to have been productive in the past, but needed work to bring mud-covered shells up to the bottom's surface.

"This is the first time we've done anything on this scale," said Pete Jensen, DNR's fisheries director, "and we hope that it'll produce positive results."

In addition to the Choptank River and Pocomoke Sound, some bagless dredging was done in St. Mary's County waters. Bagless dredging is used to scrape oyster beds to free them from silt and algae so they will grow new oysters. The men don't collect the shells, they merely "clean" them. Approximately $100,000 was spent on the effort, which was made in part to help watermen through the slack time of early spring, when their income usually falls off. About 70 boats worked in Somerset County, where the economic impact of this year's disastrous oyster season was the worst; 34 worked the Choptank and 10 in St. Mary's County.

Russell Dize praised Bobby Hambleton, the director of the program in his area. "I think everybody did an excellent job; I'm proud of the watermen," he said. We cleaned up Great Bar, France, River Bar, Lighthouse, Middle, Dawson's, and Sands by bagless dredging," he reported.

At one point it was recommended that watermen participating in the program be required to use bags on their dredges and empty them on deck so that supervisors could make sure no one was faking. This turned out to be unnecessary because watermen believed in the project and wanted to make it work.

Bagless dredging on a large scale has often been touted as a sound restoration procedure for silted-over oyster bars. The DNR's objection to bagless dredging has always been cost-effectiveness. This spring, because of money available to help watermen, bagless dredging will be given a thorough testing.

Meeting the Bitter Cold

When James and I arrive at the dock to meet Captain Robbie Wilson, 35, skipper of the ELSWORTH, it's 4:50 a.m. and there are at least two inches of snow and ice everywhere. It is dark and it is cold. As we wait for the crew and captain in the silence, an occasional pickup truck drives across the Knapps Narrows Bridge about 300 yards away. Their drivers are working on the skipjacks or related activities. They are the first ones up on the Island.

A car pulls up and a stocky man appears from behind the wheel. I realize that it is not Robbie but a crew member. I am getting anxious and as I move to meet my new comrade with enthusiasm, he silently walks past me for the ELSWORTH mumbling a weak "mornin'." We will wait in the snow off to the side of the dock. Robbie arrives about five minutes later. His greeting is friendly but reserved as we are invited on board.

"Watch your step. There's ice under the snow. You can put your things down in the cabin," he instructed. The cabin of the ELSWORTH looks like the cabin of a small sailboat: a five-foot by six-foot wide rectangle with bench seats running along the sides. There are two berths behind the seats that look like caves holding sleeping bags, oil skins, sweatshirts, gloves, and so on. In the middle of the floor is a huge ice chest holding an assortment of food. Shelves forward are stocked with spices, spaghetti, sauce, cookies, and other food. Frying pans hang by their handles on hooks set in a board. A small, four-burner stove provides heat, and Will, who looks about 50 and was the first crewman who arrived, is cooking scrapple and preparing to make French toast. He doesn't speak.

James and I start to put our gear in the port-side berth. The silence is broken: "Christ, don't put it in there. William will have a fit. Put it in the other one over there." Who's William? Is the starboard berth Will's? Is this his way of being nice? There is another forward cabin with two similar berths. There is no forward passageway. There is no toilet. I am thinking of claustrophobia when this small room is filled with six men . . . at least it's warm. There is no further conversation. I go up on deck to see Robbie.

Robbie Wilson is regarded by many watermen around the Bay as one of the best. He is a young, short, stocky man with a quick smile and rosy cheeks. Hardworking and deeply respected by his colleagues, he was born and raised on Tilghman Island. All he has ever done is work the water and he works hard to "stay ahead so he never has to do any other kind of work."

He is presently climbing into the small yawl, "push boat," which hangs from an array of davits and pulleys from the stern. Powered by a 327 Chevy engine, there is no steering mechanism. When we are about to get underway the push boat will be lowered in the water, her bow snug against the stern of the skipjack. From controls on the larger vessel, the captain will use the push boat's power to get us underway. Steering is controlled by the ELSWORTH rudder. The push boat battery is dead so Robbie must go down the road to his other workboat, BRENDA II, to get jumper cables. It's freezing and still snowing lightly at 5:15 a.m.

Minutes later a small, thin, black man appears. William has arrived! He is full of energy as he comes below and sees us. He sits next to Will. James and I sit across from them in total silence like two school boys sitting in the principal's office.

"You boys workin' on the HELLSWORTH' today? Not ELSWORTH, HELLSWORTH," he asks.

"Hope to," I say sheepishly.

"Don't mess with Robbie today, William. He'll put his foot up your ass," Will explains.

"I don't care," William responds, "I'll mess with him today just like everyday," Will cracks his first smile. There is a comradery among these men.

I think Will's initial silence is usual around strangers like us. I had experienced it before on other boats. Why are we here looking in on their world, their way of life? Do they think we're crazy for being so interested? Do we want to pry? I imagine that I am not the only one with questions. They probably have an equal number going through their minds.

"I was afraid Robbie was going to call and say get down to the boat at 2:00 this morning to go to Solomons," William says.

"I don't give a shit. I was sleeping 'til 4:00 anyway," said Will.

"Where's crew? Stevie here?"

"He might be up front. We might be a man short if the boy doesn't get down from Rock Hall with this snow."

"Why the hell don't he stay on the boat?"

Robbie is back. William cuts the conversation short, immediately gets up and moves topside. Robbie sticks his head in the cabin door and says to help ourselves to scrapple and French toast. He's waiting for Stevie to arrive and Jerome, a crewman from the MAGGIE LEE who will take the place of the fellow from Rock Hall, who probably won't show. Will doesn't speak and I'm not about to reach for a piece of anything!

William says little to Robbie. He climbs in the push boat, connects the jumper cables, and starts the engine. After the boat is in the water and lined up on the ELSWORTH's stern, he will untie her from the pilings. Robbie is at the helm. William is doing his job as Will, below, continues to do his."

When we are underway heading out of the Narrows toward the oyster bed in the Choptank River, William returns to the cabin and continues his conversation about Solomons. He picks up right where he left off 20 minutes earlier. Robbie is "out of the way" at the helm.

"Gene Tyler went to Solomons yesterday. Damn, I'm glad we didn't have to go down there," he says.

Robbie, topside at the wheel, is bundled in thick winter coveralls and listening through a small one-foot by one-foot window below the wheel that gives him access to his radios, depthfinder, compass, and switches. He says, "Gene went to Solomons following that Natural Light." I think of the spiritual awareness that must have inspired him to take the MARTHA LEWIS south in search of oysters. "Yes, sir," Robbie continues. "Miss Deenie don't let him drink at home so he follows that Natural Light every couple weeks." The men all laugh, and I am self-conscious about my thoughts—they're talking about beer and I'm getting philosophical. The jokes and jibes have started on the ELSWORTH already.

William asks Robbie, "How'd Gene do in Solomons?"

"Gene, he ain't never gonna tell."

"Well, if he stays a couple of days without coming home then he's on to somethin'."

"Or at least hopin' a lot harder," Robbie says as he moves to jibe at Jerome a little in front of me.

"He's a hell of a good crewman," he tells me within earshot of Jerome, "and I had to let him go a while back."

"You're kidding," I exclaim.

"No, I'm sure not. He didn't show up for three days in a row. Ain't that right Jerome? And I had to get another boy. I thought he left the country or was in a ditch somewhere. Come find out he's only up in Easton all tangled up with some girl," Robbie exclaims to Jerome's embarrassment, though showing a touch of pride, too. "Ain't that right, Jerome? And he tells me he couldn't get home. Hell, you could'a called me."

"Man, I was way back in the woods somewhere."

"Goddamn, it was worth it though, wasn't it, Jerome?"

William interrupts, "Beat the hell out of cullin' oysters."

"Damn right!" Jerome exclaims with a sheepish grin.

It will be an hour-and-a-half until we reach the oyster bed to be worked today. Stevie and Jerome eat and talk with Will and William. Discussions are quick paced and jovial. Occasionally they touch on the lack of oysters and, therefore, money. Because they are working today, they are happy.

After eating Jerome and Stevie move to their forward cabin to rest, William opens a Budweiser and Will finishes placing a six-inch stack of French toast and scrapple on the ice chest. We sit back and relax. You can eat with your fingers or with knife and fork . . . there's no etiquette . . . "just eat your fill because at 11:00 a.m. you will be cold and hungry." I relax after finally getting the courage among new friends to eat from their table. They have assured us, without saying a word, that we are welcome to share whatever is prepared. It is a good feeling to be with these men . . . lunch will be spaghetti.

The men can dredge for oysters under power on Mondays and Tuesdays. Wednesday through Friday are sail days but Robbie tells me they haven't sailed but three or four days all season, and last year they only sailed a total of a couple dozen days.

"If we get the weather—we can't get the crew. If we get the crew—we can't get the weather," he explained.

The end has often seemed near for the aging and shrinking fleet of tall-masted sailing vessels. Chesapeake Bay watermen have used sail since before the turn of the century to dredge oysters.

1987 to 1988 represents, to some captains, a last stand as many see the skipjacks fading slowly into history. About 1,500 skipjacks—low, wide, shallow draft vessels with tall, raking, wooden masts and large, tapered wooden spars extending forward from the bow, once worked the Chesapeake and her tributaries. There are only 17 working the season this year. At least five others didn't even bother to set sail. Many are for sale.

"I had a man, wanted to turn her into a charter yacht, slap $35,000 cash on the table to buy her. I thought about it and just couldn't do it. I don't know why, it's just I couldn't part with her. The 'For Sale' sign's still there, though," Robbie says. "This may be the last season drudgin' though. Can't afford to keep it up. We'll go to tongin', but I won't leave the water." The season runs the bone chilling course of winter . . . November 1 through March 15 for the skipjacks.

"Nothing's ever warm on the skipjacks except when you're painting them in summer," says Captain Russell Dize of the KATHRYN. "But when there's plenty of oysters, nothing much but ice stops her from going out."

X Marks the Spot

As we reach the spot where Robbie wants to begin dredging, William, Will, and Jerome are up putting on oilskins and rubber gloves. Stevie is still lying down.

"Jerome," Robbie yells. "Ask Stevie if he's going to work today or if he would like his wake-up call before lunch." The Captain's sarcasm is enough to get Stevie up without Jerome's assistance.

The men move to the dredges, and I am full of adrenalin and apprehension. I don't feel the cold. Will and William, in their oilskin coveralls, place "their" dredge on the deck; Jerome and Stevie do the same with theirs. A gasoline-powered auxiliary engine sitting amidship is used to raise and lower the dredges. The two dredges are dropped overboard and dragged simultaneously over the bottom from the port and starboard sides. The triangular, iron-framed dredges can hold at least three bushels of oysters, shells, and debris. This year there are fewer oysters with each catch. The dredges have sharp teeth on the lower edge to scoop the oysters into their netting. From the helm, Robbie can control both the push boat and the throttle for the dredge winder engine. Will uses a foot pedal on the side of the engine box to control the winding winch as well.

When Robbie is ready, he gives the crew the go-ahead and the dredges are dropped over a metal roller and into the water. They are attached to about 150 feet of ½ inch steel cable. When he wants a dredge pulled in, he tugs on a nylon cord to rev-up the power winder engine, which then begins to reel in the cable. Once the dredge is up to the roller, Will controls the final yard to the deck with his foot pedal so that he and William can grab two metal rings at either side of the base of the dredge to empty the net onto the huge culling board on deck. They will save oysters at least three inches in length, the rest get shoveled back over the side.

As I watch the men culling oysters, Robbie stays in constant touch with other captains by radio.

"Russell on the KATHRYN and Ed on the MINNIE V and I stay in close touch. Russell and I are never more than five minutes apart on most days. If there's an accident out there in this weather, a man can't last very long in the water. We watch out for each other, have to," he says.

Robbie talks to Captain Gene Tyler, he says Solomons looks like a "ghost town" and that he guessed right on beating the weather, but not the oysters. He will be home in two days with half the catch the other men get on the Choptank's Castle Haven. It is a game of risks.

"They say it was 29 below zero in South Dakota this mornin'," a captain says over the radio, "Believe I'd rather be workin' in this warm weather on this old drudge boat."

"Believe it's cold enough to freeze a fart out here this morning," comes another response over the radio.

Robbie tells me this may be his last year dredging oysters. He works seven days a week crabbing in the summer and puts aside enough money to get by in the winter. It is painful to think about selling the ELSWORTH, but "it ain't worth it for the money or the risk anymore. We're just keeping up now workin' two days a week and with no insurance, it's just too dangerous. I may do some patent tonging instead of running the skipjack."

At 8:15 a.m., the sun has been up for over an hour and it is a grey, cold morning. There are eight skipjacks working this area and they work in large circles and crosses, sometimes coming within 30 yards of each other.

Robbie will sell his oysters to Buddy Harrison's Oyster Company. "The buyers get together and work out a price. They're all about the same," he says. Oyster buyer Buddy Harrison's family has been in Tilghman and working on the water for over 100 years. He owns and operates Harrison's Oyster Company, Harrison's Chesapeake House, Country Inn, and Harrison's Sport Fishing Center, a hunting service. He is opening a $20 million Harrison's Restaurant at Pier 5 in the Baltimore Inner Harbor.

Meet Buddy

Buddy is Tilghman's "J. R. Ewing" and he wears his success well. Entering the beautiful Harrison's Chesapeake House, the closed-in porch is a virtual ego alley of pictures, newspaper and magazine articles, and recognition plaques. I am intrigued that he and his family do a tremendous amount of charity work. "With our hard work and success, I have instilled in my boys the importance of giving. In a rural area you need to help out everywhere you can if you've been fortunate. We try and do that," he says.

"The oyster business has reached a real ebb. The worst it's ever been. I used to have five trucks on the road taking oysters to South Dakota, Iowa, all through the Midwest. Now I have one truck on the road and my man drove through Pittsburgh over the holidays and brought back 60 gallons of oysters. He couldn't get rid of them. Damn if it hasn't been a time since we were in this kind of fix."

Harrison said that he is meeting "unbelievable" resistance to Maryland oysters. "Last year we had a box market in California that took 400 to 600 boxes a week. Now I can't move 'em out there because people read the news that Maryland oysters are diseased and dying. From the way the newspapers have reported these things, I might be afraid to eat a Maryland oyster myself, if I didn't know better," Harrison said. "We've always sold a lot of oysters for church dinners, but we're losing this market because of the price and because people are afraid of the disease," he added.

"We had oysters to begin with," said Larry Simns. "But all the oystermen from the lower part of the Bay [hardest hit by MSX] come up the Bay to harvest. You've got five times as many watermen working those bars."

"Everybody is going to the same places, but those places won't hold up. We've got them right now but every day they're catching less and less and less."

"The problem with oysters is MSX and Dermo," Harrison said. "But I'll tell you it's two years in a row of drought that killed it. If we have two wet summers in 1988 and 1989, I'm optimistic the oysters will come back. But the next two years will be a disaster because it will be tough getting the spat. We always have hills and valleys, but this is a real valley for this industry now."

"I have an obligation to the watermen to do what I can. Some of the skipjack captains sold product to my father 30 to 40 years ago."

"We're doing everything we can to hang in there now. The catchers are doing okay because they are making money but the packers, like my oyster company, can't get the volume to make any money as the middle man. There was a time when I bought 3,500 to 4,000 bushels a day from the catchers in all the month of January. I won't even come close to that," he said.

Buddy Harrison has worked with men on the water all his life. He is optimistic about the Chesapeake he loves so dearly. "I think the Bay is on the way back. People are eating more crabs than ever in history. Aggressive watermen who out-maneuver obstacles and use their brains, not brawn, will survive. They have to think about making money on crabs and watching their finances. Those that don't will be eaten alive. It's always tough making a living off a natural resource, so a lot gets down to using your wits. While some older watermen cry doomsday, the young ones who are smart and aggressive will make out all right, I suppose. Nobody knows what's down the road," he says.

His sons Buddy Jr. and Chucky work for him running the oyster house and the charter fishing/hunting business respectively. They were not allowed to work the water when they were teenagers. "I forbade them to go oystering. At 16 or 17, money and a car are the most important things to a boy. There was too much money for them. At $200 a day in a good year's opening season, boys would quit school in the ninth grade to get that instant gratification. I wouldn't let them do it. I made them stay in school. They went on to graduate from college and come back here to live. They were uncomfortable in the city and I'll tell you they cussed me when their high school friends had money and cars and they had to stay in school. They thank me now."

Robbie Wilson tells me buyers were paying about $25 a bushel at the beginning of the season. Then the price dropped to a mournful $17. "Our biggest day was only 107 bushels, with a limit of 150, when you take a third off the price for the boat and divide the rest in five shares for the men, it doesn't leave much for puttin' in a day's work. When the price is up to $25 a bushel, it's worth leavin' home at midnight Sunday and working 'til Tuesday night, but now it ain't worth the risk of getting caught in a winter storm. Last year, three or four times a bad storm would come on you at night, can't see anything, finally find a harbor to sneak into and ride her out."

Back to Business

We pass a blue bottle buoy in the water. There is a similar black buoy 50 yards away. "Those are marks," Robbie explains. "If you hit a good lick, mark it with a buoy. I don't throw many myself over the side 'cause then everybody flocks around it."

"I love workin' on the water. All the real watermen I know will hang in year after year no matter what happens. Like Miss Deenie says, we have good years and bad. If oysters are bad, then crabs are usually good . . . same with clams." Miss Deenie also says on the water you must be optimistic and "remember the Lord will provide." I wonder if Robbie and the crew would agree with that on a bad day.

William interrupts by yelling back, "You must be a damn fool. Wouldn't you rather be chasing a woman around the bedroom this mornin'?" I concur that the thought had crossed my mind.

"Hey, Jerome. Them white boys don't do any work on the MAGGIE LEE, do they?" Robbie yells with a smile. "Ain't worth a shit," Jerome says, laughing sarcastically. I knew immediately that the crew on the MAGGIE LEE were good friends of the men on the ELSWORTH.

The skipjack captains have the same problems as the other men who own boats; finding dependable crew. Many of the men that usually work steadily on the water have reluctantly taken jobs on shore that pay more money. There are plenty of other men looking for work, but the question is "are they dependable?"

Between dredges, a discussion starts on deck about coveralls. Jerome can't wear them to work, Stevie doesn't like them, William says he has a pair of Stevie's that Robbie found down below and said he could have them. William says he bought his "a couple of years ago—damn good ones—Sears Best." Jerome responds, "Looks like you got the 'best' of them." Laughter ends the three-minute break. James is asleep in the cabin. It's 9:30 a.m., we've been up for five-and-a-half hours, he can't get a lot of pictures now, and there will be ten more hours out here before we head in. The radio is constantly on with conversations ranging from furniture shopping, crew, skiing, 60 Minutes, the stock market, to vacations.

"I take a two-day trip to Ocean City every August with my family. That's my vacation, but this year I'll put that up to September so I can crab straight through and keep my buyer happy," Robbie says.

"Well, they're calling for a depression in 1990—better tighten up on everything," a captain says to the fleet, "Black Monday was just a little tremor—the big heart attack is coming."

"The boy might have somethin' there," is the response.

"Can't go by all the gloom and doomsayers though," says Captain Russell Dize. "We hear that every oyster season."

"Hi, Ed," Robbie calls up the MINNIE V on the radio. "I got Mick on board here and he grew up with ole' 'L.T.' (Captain Larry Thomas). Ed asks if I know L.T.'s wife, Sue, that works on the telephone lines for the phone company. "Yea, I know her real well," I said. "Well," Ed says, " I believe there must have been a hell of a man shortage in Deale for her to marry ole' 'L.T.'." All the captains laugh over the radios. The constant issue all day is the cold and ice. Other conversations are to break the monotony of these captains who will stand 12 to 15 hours at the helm with the exception of a couple of 10 to 20 minute breaks. "This is my slowest winter since becoming a waterman," Robbie says.

I believe that to be true. The decline in the Chesapeake Bay oyster harvest has been precipitous, particularly in the past five years. As recently as 1974, the nation's largest estuary produced 22.9 million pounds of oyster meat, or nearly four million bushels—52 percent of the national oyster harvest. By 1984, the Bay harvest was down to 12.5 million pounds, about two million bushels, or only just under 26 percent of the nation's harvest. The 1987 to 1988 season could be below 400,000 bushels.

Aside from the small catch due to MSX disease, the men faced new catch regulations. The start of the 1987 to 1988 oyster season was pushed back 15 days and watermen's working hours and harvest limits were cut under new regulations put out by the Department of Natural Resources.

The new regulations, which will apply through winter 1987-88 season only, were proposed by the state's Oyster White Paper Committee back on September 8th. The season began October 1 instead of September 15 and the hours for catching oysters limited from sunrise to 3 p.m. Monday through Friday. Watermen are allowed to work from sunrise to noon on Saturdays, except for the skipjack dredge boats working under power. Current regulations allow harvesting until sunset.

In addition, there will be a limit of 15 bushels per licensee, not to exceed 30 bushels per boat per day, except for power and sail dredgers (skipjacks). Current limits are 25 bushels per licensee and 50 bushels per boat.

Lunch is spaghetti. Crew talk turns to the usual subjects of drinking, women, money, and oysters. Few of the captains drink much alcohol or act rowdy at all. Most are family men deluged with worries divided between the water and the shore.

Robbie asks me at midday after we have been out for a few hours and gotten to know each other a little better, "What do you do for a living? You say you paint houses or do dry wall?"

I mentally flash to Larry Simns, my usual point of reference these days, and his comment that the only work that counts is physical work. I am caught off guard for a moment by this man who has spent over eight hours at the helm and is looking down the hour glass at seven more. I immediately recognize that writing this book is *not work* in his eyes, so my real worth must be in house painting or dry wall. I am both embarrassed and ashamed to tell this waterman that I do public relations and write for a living. For some strange reason, I feel "small" even though I, too, put in an average of 60 hours a week making a living.

"No, I write and do public relations for the marine industry," I admit, wanting to go immediately into a ten-minute dissertation in defense of my very existence on earth. I think it best, however, to cut it off. I have found these men very open and very perceptive.

"Well, I graduated from high school and never used much of it. I never even write a letter. But, if you help us with this book, I guess that will be fine," he terminates the issue leaving me with the feeling that I could reclaim a little of my self-confidence and self-esteem. I do and we are back to the subject at hand.

Captain Robbie Wilson had only been on a skipjack once before he bought the ELSWORTH in 1979. He was 12 years old and Captain Tyler of the MARTHA LEWIS took him out for the day. He never sailed. "I had her and didn't know what to do so I hired this old captain on for two weeks to show me how to set sails and how she worked. After two days, hell, he was in my way, but I promised him two weeks, so he stayed."

"When I started, Buddy (Harrison) was buying thousands of bushels a day. They are the middle men and make a couple dollars on each bushel. Now it's tough, the packers are really takin' a lickin'."

I notice that in the process of culling oysters, William and Jerome bend over their respective portion of the pile of oysters collected in the dredge bucket. With legs straight, throwing the legal oysters between their legs, without looking, into a pile behind them to their personal piles. William says, "The Captain wants to see your ass high and your head low, just like a buffalo, when you're cullin'." At the end of the day there were 61 bushels collected and each man had about 15 bushels each . . . so much for technique. All I could focus on was the degree of cold and back pain along with the number of times an hour that the 250-pound dredge bucket peered over the side with two men grabbing a steel ring to lift and flip the bucket, dumping the oysters on the culling board. At this pace, with less than half the state quota of 150 bushels collected, I figured the men stared at the dredge bucket coming over the gunwale at least 125 times each and then had to cope with 250 lbs. each time to lift and flip.

At about 4:00 p.m. Robbie tells the crew, "Keep 'em up, we're going home." William pauses to ask me if I like going out with "Captain

Midnight," the crew's term for Robbie Wilson, who will travel all night to a bed and stay out until the last minute to leave.

Dredges are unfastened and stacked neatly forward of the winder engine box. Each man shovels his pile of culled oysters against the rear and side boards and takes a bucket, full of water, to wash down the culling boards and deck. With this chore done they head for the cabin to strip wet and dirty oilskins and sweatshirts, get warm, talk and rest before reaching the dock at Harrison's Oyster Company over an hour away. Jerome and Stevie go to the forward cabin to lie down. Will, William, James, and I go to the main cabin. We have the stove. Jerome and Stevie have a kerosene heater. Robbie asks Will and William to come topside and set the sail. He wants to "race" the NELLIE T. BYRD and MINNIE V home. The crew wants him to win because they know that he who gets to the dock last unloads last and also gets home last. I pray Robbie wins the "race."

Down below I ask if anyone has ever been lost out here. "Not for some time," William says.

"Tell him when you fell overboard," Will says.

"You fell overboard?" I asked William, astonished.

"Yea, in Solomons. It was 13 degrees below zero with the wind chill and I was pushing her off the dock with a boat hook. The hook slipped and I was grabbing at all the air I could. Went right through the ice. The got me out before Robbie knew what happened, but I'll tell you I was so cold my nuts were rattlin' until they finally shriveled up to my throat!"

"Robbie went over too!" Will said making fun of the Captain. "Was fixin' the yawl and fell off her. Didn't ya', Cap?" Robbie did not respond. This was supposed to be his secret.

I go up on deck. The temperature is dropping rapidly as the Arctic front they called for is becoming a reality. Robbie shows me the lights for Tilghman Island and our course. I am more interested in how we're doing against the NELLIE T. BYRD and the MINNIE V in the "race."

We come in second and are about five minutes behind the MINNIE V. As we approach the oyster dock, William climbs into the yawl. Lights from the oyster company light up the narrows. It's pitch black otherwise. All of a sudden, 40 or so yards from the dock, the engine on the yawl stalls. We are moving at four knots, approaching the stern of the MINNIE V in a loaded down skipjack with no reverse action available. Robbie grabs the microphone and tells the MINNIE V we lost our engine, watch the stern and get someone running up the dock to catch a line. We have to tie the ELSWORTH off on a piling to stop her before there is a collision. I see a boy running through the snow to an ice-covered pier about 40 feet from our bowsprit and 65 feet from the MINNIE V, it will be just enough room, if it works. Robbie yells to Will and I to make sure we clear a couple of yachts tied alongside the approaching bulkhead and for Jerome to move forward. William is to throw our stern line ashore to the boy. William's first throw is a miss. "Goddamnit," he says.

"Come on William, we got to make her," Robbie yells. The second toss is in the boy's grasp and he ties the ELSWORTH off in seconds. Jerome is within feet of the stern of the MINNIE V. Our bowsprit is a good ten feet forward of her stern off the starboard side. We're okay and everyone nonchalantly goes about his business of getting ready to unload.

Two skipjacks can unload at the same time. Buddy Harrison, Jr. greets us. He will count the bushels that come off the ELSWORTH and work a power winder that will move large metal baskets from the shore to the deck and into which Will can shovel his pile of oysters. As each bucket fills, William puts the winch hook on it and guides it off the skipjack as Buddy, Jr. raises it with the power winder. A dock boy empties the metal basket into a wheelbarrow that another boy will wheel to a conveyor belt that lifts the oysters into the packing house truck.

When the oysters are off the boat the men take buckets with long cords attached to the handles, slip them overboard, and wash down the decks for a second time with ice water. Then they do a quick scrub with course brushes and rinse again.

The day's catch totaled 61 bushels. Each man will make about 130 dollars, or less than $10 an hour for the 14- to 15-hour day. Buddy Jr. gives Robbie a "ticket" and he can collect the money later on tomorrow. As we take the ELSWORTH back to her pier, Robbie explains that the oystermen can have up to five percent of their catch in small oysters or shell; 95 percent must be legal three-inch oysters.

"The Man gave me a ticket and took my license for 60 days one time. I got one ticket for being seven percent and two for being eight percent. I appealed to the DNR and told the hearing board in Annapolis I didn't cull the oysters. I'm doing the best I can. I fired the one boy who got me two tickets. The government man gave me a lecture about how he would hire more competent crew. I told him it wasn't like there was a line waiting to work on the boat. Larry Simns went with me and so did a packer. They suspended the 60 days for ten days. The government people don't know what it's like working out here and the thousands of shells these boys go through, and you can lose your license even after you tell them the oysters have been handled three or four times before they look 'em over."

It is about 8:00 p.m. Robbie invites me back and I accept. We all leave quietly into the night.

Miss Deenie's House

On Tuesday morning, I spent several hours talking to Miss Deenie. James was up at sunrise to take pictures. I was as quiet as could be while fixing coffee and cereal on the Tyler's summer porch. Thoughts of the previous day on the ELSWORTH and previous times spent with the people who call themselves watermen lead me to think of the many ways that Tilghman Island, for example, is really a sub-culture in our society at large. Of course, there are many sub-cultures throughout our society, but I had never really given it any thought. Perhaps subconsciously, or even consciously, we think of people or groups of people as being "different" from the norm, but the realization of this was becoming more apparent as I began to think of this particular group of people in their enclaves of Tilghman Island, Smith Island, Tangier Island, Hooper's Island, Deal Island, and so on around the Chesapeake.

"Good morning," she said shuffling through the door in bedroom slippers and robe. "Have you got coffee? Yes. Good. Now I'll fix you eggs and scrapple. You may as well eat breakfast."

"Thanks, but I don't want to put you to any trouble," I said.

"No trouble. I don't mind at all and you don't really want to eat that cold cereal anyway," Miss Deenie said.

We spent the next several hours talking about changes taking place on the Chesapeake. "When you're raised on the water like we were and the children of watermen today, you have to know that you won't see your parents, or at least your father, for days on end. For many children I know it's sad because they hate to see their fathers leave, but they grow to learn something of the water and they assume this is the way everybody lives. The children have to know that they can't have things as they want them. Our lives are dictated by what comes from the Bay, when it comes, and how much will be delivered up," she said.

I learn that many families worry for a time about their children finding work on the water and leaving hometowns for more money. Now, with declining catches and prospects for young watermen slim by old standards, they are also saddled with rising real estate costs and development.

Miss Deenie tells me of a big development firm that bought the old Tilghman Island packing house out on a small island connected by a causeway to the main island. "They told us they were going to put in a big marina for expensive yachts and build expensive waterfront homes on the farmland across the street from here. The town fought it, but it's comin','" she said. "I know we have to accept it, but it's hard when someone comes in and tells you what they're goin' to do with your town. See, country people don't fight these men too much because we don't really understand until it's too late. And, we believe too much all the nice things they tell us and it's just not our nature. You just work hard and try to get along. If you don't get along with somebody, then stay clear of them. They told us we had 'a choice' of about fifty $300,000 homes or a whole lot of cheaper homes. My brother Russell, says we might as well have the $300,000 homes . . . at least they won't be so many," she concludes.

"Funny thing about outsiders movin' onto the Island is they move here for second homes or to retire to get away from the city hassles and enjoy the quiet of our community. Then they come tell us when our kids make noise riding their bikes or cars up the roads. They expect life to be 100 percent different here, and too bad, it isn't."

On January 7, 1988, the Chesapeake region, like the rest of the mid-East was hit with an Arctic front holding temperatures in the teens. On January 8, 6 to 8 inches of snow fell. Tilghman was snowed in, visibility on the water was measured in hundreds of yards rather than miles and the Choptank River, where the skipjack captains have

Your face
        marks the passage of time
as you follow your mind's eye
to search
        through the catch culling
                silently
                swiftly

Your face
        traces many passages
        with hope
        and
        optimism that there will be
a time and passage
        upon this Bay
        for your
        tomorrow.

MSB

nurtured a stretch of healthy oysters, was covered with a layer of ice, the first of the year. I decided to stay in Annapolis and prepare for the start of the 1988 Maryland General Assembly session. I have been working with Larry Simns and the Maryland Watermen's Association to exclude federally documented commercial workboats from the Maryland Boat Excise Tax and exclude out-of-state exhibitors in the upcoming Maryland Watermen's Exposition from having to fuss with the Department of Natural Resources about getting traders licenses and posting a bond. I will leave Annapolis on Wednesday, January 13, and go over to meet with Captain Russell Dize on the skipjack KATHRYN.

"That ain't blood, man, that boy has got the Choptank River runnin' in his veins."

More Waterman Wisdom

On January 11 and 12, with the Choptank oyster beds under ice, several of the skipjack captains take to the ice-free open waters of the Chesapeake to search for scattered beds that might not have been annihilated by MSX. Those beds are few and far between and, even though these are "push" days, the 10 to 13 degree temperatures, the ice closing in, and the Arctic front holding on makes it rough. The market is up a little to $22 a bushel, so this makes it more palatable. The goal for the captain is still in the 60 bushel range, well below the limit of 150 bushels.

As I drive across the Chesapeake Bay Bridge early on the 13th, there is a congregation of some 15 clam boats off Sandy Point State Park and three off the Westinghouse site a half-mile away. The men managed to break through the ice as they came from the open Bay into the shallower clamming areas, but they would still have to work in close proximity to each other. To stray from the already broken ice means risking ice breaking through a wooden hull and a lost boat and wet crew. It's safer and wiser to stay together and keep already broken ice moving about as much as possible. With the temperature well in the teens and winds from 15 to 25 mph, the boats off Sandy Point are somewhat sheltered. As I drive past, I look for Crow on DAWN and

Larry on DAWN II and, for a moment, I think about the sympathetic reaction of the Washington Redskins fans when they learned their beloved 'Skins, in the NFL playoff game with the Bears, would be playing on Chicago's Soldier Field with temperatures hovering around 14 degrees for the three-hour contest. Today, the "teams" of the DAWN II and other clammers would play a game with the Chesapeake Bay for at least 12 hours and the wind chill index taking temperatures well below 0° F. I believe I'd rather be playing football in Chicago!

I have four goals in mind for this day: spend time with oyster packer Buddy Harrison, Captain Russell Dize, Brenda and C. R. Wilson, and waterman Jack Koenerman. I drive down to the ELSWORTH to see if Robbie or anyone is around. No luck.

I decide to go to Buddy Harrison's Chesapeake House to talk to him and use a telephone. Buddy is free and we chat for an hour about the state of the oyster business and the threatening issue of packing houses shutting down and the people who shuck oysters being out of work. He is hopeful of two things. First, the government might help the packing houses economically by buying them and leasing them back to former owners, and second, Maryland's oyster industry might get some federal assistance if it's declared a state of emergency. Both hopes are months away from a response. Buddy is working on his major restaurant project in the Baltimore Inner Harbor, so I excuse myself with the hopes of returning later in the day after meeting with Dize and Wilson.

As I leave to track down Captain Dize, the ice breaker BIG LOU is opening up a channel through the Narrows and into the harbors. Three tonging boats are working in the ice-free channel. They will tong for a few more hours and then get back to the packing house before the ice closes in again.

Russell Dize and his family live in a nice brick house overlooking the Choptank River. I am greeted warmly by this fourth-generation waterman and invited into the living room, a living room decorated in much the same fashion as Captain and Mrs. Tyler's: memorabilia and pictures of skipjacks, races, family, and in Russell's case, autographed pictures of President Ronald Reagan's visit to the Eastern Shore and a framed personal letter from the President to Russell. He takes a moment to show me a collection of clay pipes, Indian axes and hatchets, bottles, arrowheads, and shark's teeth accumulated from dredging the

Bay. He has had a friend from the Smithsonian date several stone axes
to 5,000 years ago. The clay smoking pipes are 18th century. Russell
explains each one and is obviously very proud of the fascinating arti-
facts. I am amazed at the collection and think of the people who were
here before us. They had an endless bounty and we are watching it disappear in less than 300 years.

As we sit on the sofa, Russell speaks quickly and seriously. He has
served as vice president of the Maryland Watermen's Association and
was one of the founders 15 years ago. "I told them I would be vice president, but if Larry ever quits, don't come to me. I won't do it. That
man has given up his family, time on the water, and a lot of personal
money," he says of his friend. I am reminded of Governor Schaefer
saying Larry Simns is "the quiet hero of the State of Maryland."

"The oyster industry is in bad shape, but it hasn't bottomed out yet.
It will get worse. Next winter won't be worth going out at all for most
men. One of the reasons we're all getting by this year is because we
haven't spent any money on our boats. With low harvest, we just main-
tained our boats and equipment. Nothin' extra. Now, next season, the
boats will be worse off and so will the oysters. You tell me?" he asked.

"If we have a wet spring, we can wash the MSX back out of the Bay,
but see, we're on a three-year oyster cycle and we have lots of small oysters but most all are dead. We'll be lucky to get 185,000 bushels this
winter and that's a far cry from 1.5 million."

Russell owns RDS Seafood on Tilghman and runs two more clam
boats while he captains the KATHRYN. He buys oysters and clams
from other watermen and sells them to markets along the East Coast.
He, too, worries about the packing houses and shuckers. "When they
go out of business, like they're doin' now, what will happen when oysters come back? We'll be hurt because the houses will be down. It's a
mess. And, then you combine this stuff with the fact that we can't get
insurance on the skipjacks, or it's too expensive. Why, five or six
months insurance for $100,000 cost me $12,000 a year. And without
money to pay good crew, we get men doing the job because they can't
do anything else. My boys are all from Crisfield . . . at least they're
watermen," he says in a tone less than enthusiastic.

As a fourth-generation waterman, Russell Dize says, "I swore I
would never drudge when I was back in high school. I wouldn't fool

with skipjacks. Here I am. It's in my blood and I don't want the skip-jacks to go. I think as long as I see 'em I think there's hope."

What hurt the men working on the water, according to Russell Dize and other colleagues, does not have to do with the Bay as a natural re-source. It has to do with politics. In the early 1970's, the State of Maryland reorganized the makeup of the Maryland General Assembly and how many Delegates or Senators an area, or district might have to represent constituents. This reapportionment, based on population, cut severely into the amount of political clout that watermen could carry off in the Maryland State House. "We used to carry the votes on legislation because we had all the Eastern Shore, St. Mary's County, Calvert County, Charles County, and a few others. Now the urban counties like Montgomery, Baltimore, and Baltimore City outnumber our votes and they're not real sympathetic to us 'cause they don't un-derstand our troubles. We don't have the clout anymore," he says.

Larry Simns agrees. "Politics is how we used to get a lot done. Now, with the committees made up of many liberal activist legislators, we have a harder time of it. See, when a rural county elects people to of-fice, that man is known in the county and he knows the issues and people by name. All of Kent County has the number of people Annapolis City does, so you see how personal things are here. Hell, it's a prestige job in the country but it's probably the lousiest job there is in a place like Montgomery County. We're just hurt by the whole damn thing," he said.

Russell says that he hopes government won't impose many restric-tions for the sake of protection because "when it all comes back, the restrictions on harvesting will be on and the legislators won't lift them. They don't change easy.

"It's the same with development. It's hard to fight pollution with so many people wantin' to move in. Hurricane Agnes took all the grasses, and development will keep them gone. If a man comes along and says I'm building 80 expensive homes or 300 less-expensive homes, I don't want either but I'll take the lesser of the two evils," he said. "These people move in and now we have 'recreational' watermen and sport fishermen competing with us just tryin' to make a livin'. The 'recrea-tional' watermen have other jobs; we don't. And the fishing people would like to ban commercial fishing altogether."

"I do think it can turn around. What worries me, though, is we used to crab so we could oyster. Now, we oyster so we can crab. It's turned reverse. Oyster was always king here. Now, we just get by. We crab as long as we can because now they're there in the Bay. But watermen don't do anything to help themselves. They won't go to meetings . . . nothing unless their backs are up against the wall . . . then it's too late. They don't want to bother with it. They want it the way it was 30 or 50 years ago, as if there's never a change.

"It costs me about $10,000 a year to keep a working skipjack. I have insurance and expenses on two clam boats. The boys who grow up on the water, it's in 'em to stay here but they can't afford it. If it gets good again, then men will be back. A man hates to leave the water when it's in his blood.

"Why, we have more fish, crabs, seafood being eaten than ever before, but a good crab potter will have to lay 800 to 1,000 pots to make a living, and 75 percent of his money will go for expenses. After this oyster season, bad as it is, there will be no free time and workin' seven days a week to do crab pottin'. A good man might make $25 to $30,000—he better—it's about the only thing left." Russell Dize said.

Captain Dize doesn't drink and attends church regularly. His daughter, Lea, is a graduate of Old Dominion University and is a dental hygienist in Virginia Beach. Captain Dize says, "There's not much work for her here anymore."

His son Rusty is a junior at St. Michaels High School. Rusty is an honor student who wants to be a lawyer. Captain Dize attributes Rusty's academic success to the fact that "he's never been allowed to work the water and I tried to suppress his interest in my boats all his life. He can work in my hardware store but not on my boats. Once they get a taste of the temporary money, they quit school, and they have a tough life ahead of 'em. I was eight years old and on a boat, and by the tenth grade I could run a clam boat by myself on Smith Island. I was 18 and owned my first clam rig, and made $8,000 in the first three months and thought I was rich and in heaven. Not Rusty. He's goin' the better way. My wife keeps the books and can tell you to the penny what college cost us for Lea. A lot, I'll tell ye. And I'll keep pushin' 'till Rusty is through. It's in me to sail a drudge boat. I love sailing, but I've sadly tried to keep my son away from it all."

Skipjack captains build and weld dredges for their own boats themselves. They have to keep expenses down. Russell Dize and Robbie Wilson will get together and work to make the job easier. There are five different dredges used on a skipjack and the dredge a captain selects depends on the consistency of the Bay bottom he and his crew will be working. For sandy bottoms they use "gummers" which have no teeth' for clay and sand mixture bottoms they use "tooth gummers"; for shell, rock-hard bottoms, working an edge of fine or hard material, or mud bottom they use long teeth dredges. In the course of a day, the dredges can be changed by crew in a matter of seconds by simply undoing a shackle.

Russell and many of the other captains will forget oystering and go to work for the State the first week of April catching and hauling seed oysters. They can catch about 800 bushels in just over an hour off of a designated seed bar and then haul them up the Bay to where the State instructs them to shovel the oysters overboard. They get paid by the bushel and load the mighty skipjacks until they sit low in the water. It helps to plant a new natural oyster bed for future growth. "The four men on KATHRYN worked five days a week for four or five weeks last year. It's not bad. No culling; just dredge, move, and dump. It's supplemental income while we wait for crabs," Russell says.

In the midst of what promises to be a season that will see a record low harvest of oysters in Maryland, Talbot County waterman Jack Koenerman refuses to give way to gloom and doom .

Long known as one of Talbot County's top clammers, as well as for his forceful language and frank opinions, Jack believes in going full steam in pursuit of a living and playing hard when he has the time. Even though Maryland's seafood industry is having hard times just now, Jack displays more than a little impatience with watermen who are overcome with pessimism.

Since he was discharged from the Army in 1960, Jack has been working on the water, and he's seen worse times than these. "When I got out of the Army and went to work hand tonging, you had to work from sunup to sundown for six bushels of oysters, and you got maybe $2.50 or $3.00 for them. The fellows who want to work, the ones who'll bust their butts, they'll make out just fine around here."

The first half of the day Jack spends clamming in the Bay off Kent

Island where he keeps his clam boat—about a 100-mile round trip—if he doesn't have to carry his clams somewhere else on the way back. Buying oysters in the afternoon is the second half of his working day. When he finishes with the clams, he drives to Neavitt to buy oysters from men he's worked around and has lived near all his 27 years on the water.

Days are long for Jack, but they've shortened considerably from this last summer when he had to chase his own market for clams and drive long distances to meet the trucker who carried them to his customers. Sometimes the meeting place was along U.S. 301, sometimes as far away as Crisfield. "I was running 18- or 20-hour days for a solid month there, but sometimes that's what you've got to do to make a living. Being a waterman is no 40-hour-a-week job," he added. "Some people get into this business and don't treat it like a business," he said. "Maybe they think it's more of a pasttime, but you can't think that way and make a living.

"I don't care if we have MSX or what, if there's anything at all and a man's willing to work hard to get it, he can make a living on the water. Often it's a matter of searching out a new market, or doing a sales job and making one. Watermen can't depend on things remaining the same, season to season or even week to week. Scarcity and variable markets are always a threat to a waterman's livelihood and his only defense against them is hard, smart work."

Meet C.R.

On most afternoons, a half an hour after school, he can tell you how most of the watermen did working earlier in the day, where they made their catches, what the market was, and what time his father will be at the dock with his own catch. He has spoken to the skipjack captains by radio, mingled with the watermen at Gary's and argued with his mother about doing his homework before he's off to meet his dad. He is C.R. Wilson, 13 years old, a smooth talker, "cute as a button," and "a real waterman."

C.R. is the son of Brenda and Robbie Wilson and the brother of nine-year-old Jason. His family has lived off the water for generations and, "come hell or high water," according to people in Tilghman, "this boy will be a heck of a waterman." His mother, Miss Brenda, has invited me over to the Wilson home to talk to C.R. It is an occurrence that I will come to enjoy with some regularity.

As we sit at the dining room table on January 12, he appears as any healthy 13 year old; long bangs hanging down over a cherubic face as he fiddles with the placemat in anticipation of my questions. "Why do you want to be a waterman?" I ask feeling self-conscious about posing such a stupid question to this boy.

"I like it. No, I love it. I don't want no lay-in job," he says with a smile.

"You're in school at St. Michaels. Do you like it? Will you finish?"

"It's a hard opinion to finish high school," he responds as his mom nods her head in affirmation. C.R. picks up her movements and offers, "Probably finish but no way for college."

His father, Captain Robbie Wilson comes in, greets me with reserved warmth and sits at the table with us. He will remain quiet unless I look at him for a response, but it is clear that I am in his home to talk to his son. Brenda adjourns to the living room. C.R. will fluctuate between calling his father "Dad" or "Rob" depending on the subject and his own self-confidence when addressing him as a parent or as a "colleague."

C.R. began crabbing with his grandfather and clamming with Robbie at six years old. Robbie tells me, "Both boys went on the water from six or seven. Brenda would call 'em once at 3:30 or 4:00 in the morning. If they got up they went; if they didn't, they missed out."

"Boy, didn't I have to deal with him then," Brenda interjects. "He'd miss going out with his father and cry and tantrum all morning. He won't get up for school, but to go on the water he only needs to be called once."

He worked and saved $2,500 when he was 11 and bought his own boat, HARD ROLLER. "I sold her to a teacher at school, and Bunky Miller built my new boat. Her name's TUFF e 'NUFF. She's 31 feet long and 10½ feet wide. Use her for crabbin'," he says.

"One day when he was 11, his grandfather, uncles, and I were workin' and he was in HARD ROLLER. I looked up and he was nowhere in sight. I drove all over the river lookin' for him and I couldn't call into Brenda because I was supposed to be lookin' out for him. 'Bout 4:00, he comes back with 20 bushels of crabs. He and another boy weren't satisfied and went up to St. Michaels, talked to a man workin' the water up that way, decided to try their luck and stayed," Robbie says with some pride and astonishment at recounting the tale.

"He has to take another boy with him because we don't want him out there alone. But, he hates payin' the boy $40 a day for crew wages."

"This summer I'm going alone. I'm 13," C.R. says emphatically.

"No you're not," Brenda speaks up.

"Ain't that just like a woman, Rob," C.R. exclaims. "Treatin' a man like a sissy. She tells me wear your life jacket and she gave me a knife. Said 'keep this in your pocket in case you get caught up in the line'. I said if it's in my pocket and I get caught up, how am I supposed to reach the knife?" We all enjoyed his humor.

C.R. is responsible for his own crab business. He finished paying off 'TUFF e 'NUFF in late January. When crabbing starts for him, "the day after school's out," C.R. will catch his own crabs, pay all his own bills and crew, set his trot lines, and be responsible for his own boat and business. He will receive little help from his father except for mechanical or electrical failures. Robbie will be running 900 to 1,000 crab pots of his own.

"The first summer he crabbed on his own, my cousin Gary, up at the store, gave him credit like the other men. When he collected his money at the end of the week, I told him to walk over to Gary's and settle up his accounts for the line and materials he put on credit to start off. C.R. walked up to the counter with a fist full of money, gave it to Gary to take what he was owed. Gary gave him back about $7.50 and C.R.'s eyes shot open. He said 'Damn, if I wasn't gettin' a family discount in here I'd be out of business!' He cracked all the men in the store up that day."

In the winter, C.R. will dredge oysters with his father during the Christmas holidays on the ELSWORTH. He worked every day the boat went out. His brother Jason goes with his uncle Charlie. "I don't want to run a skipjack. Too many responsibilities with crew and they want to know you can find oysters. When I'm 18, I want a bigger boat for a patent tong rig," C.R. says.

"From the first grade I knew I lost C.R. to the water," Brenda says. "It's in him and he'll be good like his father. His teachers even knew it back then. If there was a class discussion on something, C.R. would always want the class to change to water topics. I'm petrified when he's on the boat and down to the dock every day he's out, watchin' for him to come in. Robbie put a radio on his boat so the men know where he is. That helps," she says.

"We get him to use a buyer on the water so Robbie doesn't fool with C.R.'s crabs. It's his business. He won't sell his peelers to me. He sells 'em to a buyer who pays him cash then and there, instead of his own mother," Miss Brenda jokes easily with C.R.

"Well, you want to hold it for me and I want it then," C.R. responds in defense. C.R. is getting tired and I have to leave for home. He gets up and goes to his bedroom to his Atari game. As I get up to leave, Robbie asks if I don't want to stay a bit longer. I am thrilled with the invitation because I continually try to be sensitive to their brief private times together as a family. We sit at the table and talk about crabbing and the Bay for another hour. It's time to head for Annapolis. I must work the General Assembly with Larry Simns in the morning, a thought far removed from Tilghman Island.

Diving for Oysters

While on the skipjacks, I witnessed oysters leaving the Bay by the "boat load" and the dredging method of collecting huge quantities of oysters quickly has caused some conflict not only with the preservationists, but within the ranks of the watermen themselves. As Larry Simns pointed out, the watermen are not always working together. In oystering, there always have been conflicts over good oyster rocks between the skipjack dredges, the shaft tongers, the patent tongers, and most recently, a new breed of divers. Recently, many of the conflicts have been resolved, but I wanted to learn more from the tongers' and divers' perspective.

In recent years, a number of men have turned to diving for oysters. In theory, this method is the obvious one; the diver simply goes down to the oysters, picks them up, puts them into a basket, and takes them back to his boat. Because he can be selective, this method generally yields prime oysters, and many divers sell to raw bars and restaurants that will pay a premium for these top-of-the-line shellfish.

In practice, diving is difficult and dangerous if not practiced with skill and care. The water is very cold, necessitating a wet suit. Bay waters are cloudy, even in winter, and visibility is limited.

The diver works with a partner on the boat, who holds him tethered on a safety line and tends the compressor that pumps air down to him. The boatman also handles the line that is used to raise the oyster basket. Often a younger diver teams up with an older, experienced waterman who has a good boat and knows his waters well.

Gary Lee Fairbanks of Tilghman started diving for oysters in 1979 when few men on the Bay thought about the profession that required going beneath the Bay's surface in the dead of winter for hours at a time.

He and his partner, Mark Litchenberger, would dive in three-hour shifts. Wearing wetsuits with air pumped in to keep dry, warm, and buoyant, the divers would hang the basket around their neck and shoulder and stay down until it was full of prime oysters. The basket line was their only means of communication during a dive. The longer they worked together, the more the line became a silent umbilical cord. Through it, each could tell how the other felt—sullen, contemplative, just fooling around—by the way the line was tugged.

Their underwater "Morse Code" was fairly simple. Two tugs from the diver meant his bushel was full, haul it up. One tug from the partner on board meant another basket was coming down. Floating slightly above bottom, the diver hung the basket round his neck, leaving both hands free to gather oysters. The system proved quite profitable.

After several years, however, Gary Lee began to dive six hours a day, taking other crewmen topside. Although he enjoyed the peaceful solitude underwater, the long seasons (from the middle of October until the end of March) finally began to take their toll physically. The work began to have an impact. It had generally been assumed there would be no residual nitrogen build-up in the body when diving above 30 feet, even for extended periods of time. That theory proved wrong.

"The nitrogen build-up never had time to completely get out of my system," Gary Lee says. Because of the prolonged time he would spend underwater—six hours a day, season after season—small amounts of pressure did build up in his joints. He reluctantly called it quits in January 1987.

"The last three months I dove, my right knee sounded like a board cracking every time I bent it," he says, still wincing at the memory.

In the end, it didn't really matter. The oysters were dying out in the Bay anyway. When Gary Lee had first begun diving at North Point or at Sages Marsh, north of Claiborne, there were numerous beds waiting to be harvested. Now, he says, there isn't a live oyster out there.

Barry "Bearcat" Coleman is captain of a dive boat and works with a very competitive diver, Pat Bilbrough of Ridgely, Maryland.

If money is proportionate to the amount of effort put into earning it, Bilbrough shows that the theory works. He told Chuck Doherty of The Capital newspaper in Annapolis, "I could make $13,000 to $15,000 a year as an accountant. I can make that much in six months as a diver." He works eleven hours a day underwater with nobody to talk to except bubbles, he said.

When he surfaces, he asks Coleman, "How many have I got? What time is it? How many does everybody else have? Bragging rights are worth about as much as the money," he said.

Tonging: Another Perspective

"More primitive than dredging under sail are the long-handled oyster tongs ("shaft tongs"), scissor-like tools with rake heads that are used primarily in shallower waters and in the rivers. Shaft tongs date back to the Indians. The work is hard physical labor, and a pair of tongs only covers a very limited area. A good shaft-tonger is an artist, working entirely by feel at depths from ten to over thirty feet. "He earns his money," says John Page Williams.

Boats will have several different shaft lengths to chose from, depending on the depth of the water they are working. The tongers work the currents and when they have a catch they will place them on a culling board for another crew member to sort through, keeping the legal-size oysters.

A variation on shaft tongs is the patent-tong rig, invented and patented on Solomons Island, Maryland, in the 1930's. This includes a large set of tong (rake) heads, operated mechanically from a mast and boom, usually on a larger boat than those used by the shaft (hand) tongers. Even so, each can only work a relatively small area at a time.

The principal is the same as hand tonging, only more efficient, of course. A hydraulic winch lowers the mechanical tong rig onto the water and retrieves it back with a catch of oysters for the culling or sorting aboard.

The oyster season in Maryland officially ends on April 1st. Bert Kappel, owner of Annapolis Seafood, said last year he catered 14 oyster roasts. He didn't do one this year. "I couldn't give them away," he exclaimed.

The Red Lobster Restaurant seafood chain, for example, refused to buy Maryland shellfish until the Interstate Shellfish Sanitation Conference (ISSC) approved the state's management plan. This kind of embargo cut severely into the jugular of the waterman's cashflow. And, in the opinion of many observers, it will take more than the ISSC decision to increase the public's acceptance and appetite for oysters.

On Kent Narrows, George Harris, manager of Fisherman's Seafood Market said, "We need to build public confidence in our shellfish. The more understanding the public has, the more confidence they'll have in seafood. We've virtually shut down our oyster production, and it's not over yet."

LADIES OF THE BAY
A Song by Dody Welsh Parris

A hundred years ago their sails filled the winter sky.
White against the slatey grey, they almost seemed to fly.
Shoresmen called them skipjacks and loved to brag how they
Had never seen their likes for pulling oysters from the Bay.

> Ladies of the Bay, they were proud ladies of the Bay.
> I chant their names soft to myself on a winter's day.
> Rebecca Ruark, Stanley Norman, Ketherine, Caleb Jones.
> Their names ring out a chorus that echoes in my bones.

Patent tongs and diesels were the wonder of their day.
No one had time for sailing but rich men out to play.
Now fiberglass don't look like wood, but it's easier any day.
And it's hard enough to make ends meet from the waters of the
Bay.

> Chorus

Now some have been abandoned, long forgotten in a marsh,
Timbers all 'arotten, barnacles in their spars.
Some will carry tourists out for a holiday.
And just a few are dredging still—proud ladies of the Bay.

> Chorus

Shoveling oysters on the skipjack to make sure they are piled high and evenly distributed on both sides of the vessel.

William washes the deck of the Elsworth after a twelve-hour day of dredging.

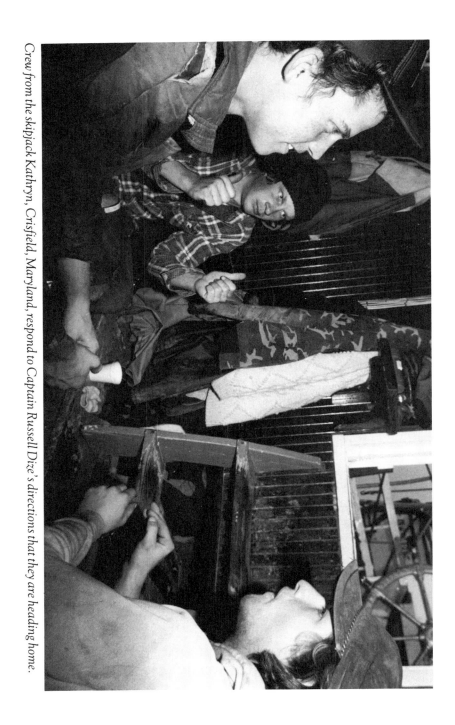

Crew from the skipjack Kathryn, Crisfield, Maryland, respond to Captain Russell Dize's directions that they are heading home.

Will fixes spaghetti and meatsauce aboard the Elsworth for lunch. It's 5:30 a.m.

Crew of the Kathryn furling the main sail.

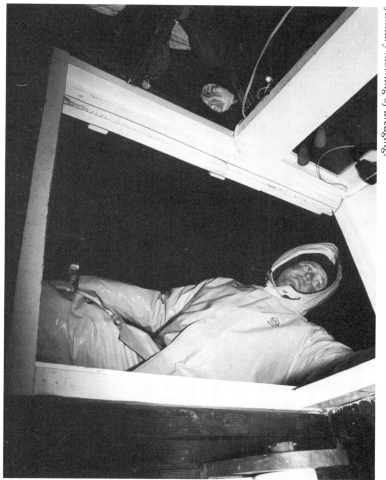

Captain Russell Dize on the Kathryn checks below during a snowstorm at 4:30 on a cold January morning of dredging.

Captain William Cummings places oysters on the Pa's Pride culling board.

"Some environmentalists and scientists are alright, but too many of 'em learned everything from books and then they make regulations which the watermen don't understand. We live through the cycles. Everything goes in cycles. That's the way nature is . . . so if the oysters is off, then we try to make up for it with crabs . . . like that."

chapter 3

off the water

Making Laws

The Maryland General Assembly opened January 13, 1988, for a 90-day session. Several recreational boating laws were being considered along with the numerous laws and regulations that would affect Maryland Watermen. I had told Larry Simns I would help with two or three pieces of legislation. I told the watermen of Tilghman I wouldn't be back for a couple of weeks.

On January 15, my request to address the Anne Arundel County Delegation was granted. I sought the delegation's sponsorship on several bills and I also wanted them to consider at least one for the Maryland Watermen's Association. Larry met me outside the delegation hearing room at 9:15 a.m.

In 1986, the Maryland General Assembly passed, and the governor signed into law, the Maryland Boat Excise Tax. The law stated that any boat sold in Maryland had to pay the Department of Natural Resources a 5% excise tax. I worked on the original legislation, and it was widely supported by the boating community because the tax collected went into the Waterway Improvement Fund instead of the usual State General Fund. A member of the Anne Arundel County Delegation, Delegate Elizabeth Smith, an avid sailor and racer with her husband Dr. Edward Anderson, was our chief sponsor of the original bill. When the original law passed on July 1, 1986, it was our intent to allow reciprocity for taxes paid in home states for boaters coming from out-of-state so that they wouldn't be hit with 5% more when they came into Maryland waters. We also intended to exclude commercial watermen from the Excise Tax. Unfortunately, the State eliminated both of these provisions, so Larry and I would testify on both items separately. The delegation was very sympathetic to Larry's position, and Delegate Smith and Chairman John Astle were infuriated that the watermen might have to pay such a tax. Larry showed the letter from the DNR stating that the tax was also retroactive for several years and that interest and penalties were being assessed on the fair market value of the boats. Delegate Astle said that the Delegation would vote on sponsoring a bill for the watermen on January 21. Larry would be at the Maryland Watermen's Association Expo in Ocean City, so we decided I would go to the voting session.

After we made our presentation on the Excise Tax Bill, Delegate Ray Huff from northern Anne Arundel County and three colleagues brought up a bill to restrict crab pots in Maryland rivers. The legislation stemmed from the fact that when the state dredged around Hart-Miller Island outside of Baltimore, the commercial watermen lost their ability to place crab pots in the area of the Island. In return for this loss, the Department of Natural Resources said the men could place pots in the Patapsco River. This satisfied the watermen, who by law are not allowed to crab pot in Maryland rivers. It didn't, however, satisfy waterfront residents who said the pots created a safety hazard for boaters. They wanted the pots removed. This single issue, which illustrates the need for watermen to work and the position taken by waterfront residents, would be a major area for debate and often confrontation between the two sides which often turned to incredible screaming matches. The legislation died in Committee and was not signed into law.

On Monday, January 18, Larry and I met with DNR Secretary Torrey Brown to discuss the Excise Tax issue. Legislation is taking more time now than actually working on the water. Torrey Brown was very upset that he had to "enforce the law on watermen" but said that he "would support the legislation to correct the situation."

A second issue to deal with was that, by law, the DNR required exhibitors for the MWA Expo to have dealer licenses and post a $2,000 bond to exhibit in the show. The DNR letter that had been sent to exhibitors also stated that they had to collect sales excise tax for boats sold at the show but delivered out of state. Three exhibitors had already backed out of the Expo because of the hassles and confusion over the sales/excise tax. Secretary Brown said that he, once again, had to enforce the law but that he would make it very easy for exhibitors to get the license and to demonstrate that they had bonding capability and that he would clarify the taxing issue. He wanted no problems, and he assured us that the marine police would not evict any exhibitor from the Expo for not having proof of a bond. Things could be "worked out." Larry and I left Secretary Brown's office two hours later feeling remotely optimistic and slightly suspicious. Time would tell, it was five days before the watermen's Expo was to open.

As people who deal with politicians and legislators know, work on each proposed piece of legislation requires many hours of lobbying to compromise, gain support, educate, or simply form a liaison. Larry Simns is the watermen's lobbyist and a truly effective individual in the game of Maryland politics. As Russell Dize said, however, the political game in Maryland as in other states is changing for the watermen.

"We lost out when the state put in reapportionment. Before that, we controlled enough votes with legislators from rural areas. Now the big city and off-the-water counties have more votes, and it's an uphill battle. This really hurt us. The other thing that hurt is the community activists, housewives, environmentalists, and educators who ran for office and won. They don't understand business, for one thing, and least of all the waterman and his problems. The big environmental group can work on 'em day and night while we're out working on the Bay, and we're losing. Like every time there is a shallow harvest for a product, the state and environmentalists yell moratorium, the watermen say wait, it's a natural cycle; the delegates support the moratorium. I'm not saying it's wrong all together, but there aren't enough ears turned our way to get the whole story," Larry said.

Proposed Legislation

The following represent proposed legislation in the 1988 Session of the Maryland Assembly that specifically affects the watermen's capability to make a living off the Bay and her tributaries:

HB 85—   Oysters—Somerset County—Power Dredging
For the purpose of extending for a certain period of time the termination date under which a person may catch oysters with a power dredging license in certain waters of the State that lie contiguous to Somerset County. SUPPORT. Governor signed into law.

HB 95—   Theft from Leased Oyster Bottoms—Penalties
For the purpose of requiring the Department of Natural Resources to bring a criminal action for theft against a person catching, destroying, or transferring oysters on an oyster bottom leased by another person; requiring the Department to revoke certain licenses of a person convicted of theft of oysters from a leased oyster bottom; and providing a mandatory minimum and discretionary maximum time before which the Department of Natural Resources may reissue certain licenses; and generally relating to penalties for catching, destroying, or transferring oysters on oyster bottoms leased by another person. OPPOSE because leased bottoms are often not marked clearly and harvesting can be done by mistake. Governor signed into law.

HB 191— Tidal Fish License-Noncommercial Crabbing
For the purpose of authorizing the Department of Natural Resources to issue a separate tidal fish license for noncommercial crabbing with a certain term; providing that noncommercial crabbing for a certain commission; providing that noncommercial crabbing license numbers need not be displayed; providing that certain noncommercial crabbing licenses issued through a certain date shall be valid for a certain period; and generally relating to the establishment of a separate tidal fish license for noncommercial crabbing. OPPOSE. Bill died in Committee.

HB 295— Tidal Fish Licenses—Delay in Application Process
For the purpose of establishing certain requirements after a certain date for obtaining a tidal fish license to catch crabs with a certain number of crab pots, finfish, oysters, or clams; providing for a delay of a certain time period in the application process for a tidal fish license under this Act; providing for the scope and application of this Act; requiring a certain application and registration process; prohibiting certain tests; and generally relating to the establishment of a delay in the application process for a tidal fish license to catch crabs with a certain number of

crab pots, finfish, oysters, and clams. SUPPORT because it delays entry by newcomers who don't make a full-time living on the water. Governor signed into law.

HB 297— Oil and Gas—Chesapeake Bay, Its Tributaries, and Other State Waters
For the purpose of requiring the Board of Public Works at certain times to select the Secretary of Natural Resources to prepare certain statements of the environmental, fiscal, and economic impact of a proposed lease in certain State water; providing for strict liability for damages that occur in the exploration, drilling, production operations, or plugging of oil or gas wells in certain State waters; and generally relating to exploration, drilling, production operations, or plugging oil and gas wells in the Chesapeake Bay, its tributaries, and other waters of the State. OPPOSE. Governor signed into law.

HB 313— Oil and Gas Drilling in Chesapeake Bay
For the purpose of prohibiting a person from drilling for oil or gas in the waters of the Chesapeake Bay or its tributaries. SUPPORT because the watermen do not want oil exploration in the Bay. Governor signed into law.

HB 538— Somerset County-Oysters-Power Dredging
For the purpose of including certain areas of Somerset County within the requirements that a person may catch oysters by power dredge only during certain time periods of the power dredging season; and making this Act contingent on the passage of another Act. SUPPORT to allow for more efficient oyster harvesting. Governor signed into law.

HB 701— Oysters—Emergency Assistance Loan Program
For the purpose of creating an Emergency Assistance Loan Program; providing for eligibility requirements under this Act; prohibiting a loan under this Act from exceeding a certain amount under certain conditions; allowing certain persons to borrow certain amounts of money under this Act; requiring the Department of Natural Resources to adopt regulations to carry out this Act; and making this Act an emergency measure. SUPPORT. Bill died in Committee.

HB 748— Aquaculture
For the purpose of promoting the development of the aquaculture industry in this State; establishing an Aquaculture Advisory Committee; defining aquaculture as an agricultural activity in this State; authorizing the Department of Natural Resources to adopt regulations to issue permits and inspect aquaculture operation; allowing the sale of striped bass or hybrids of striped bass by a certain date or upon certain

Legislative Policy Committee approval; and generally relating to the development of the aquaculture industry. OPPOSE because watermen have taken a position against the aquaculture concept. They will lose bottom land and their territory for harvest. Governor signed into law.

HB 843— Establishment of an Oyster Divers' Advisory Committee and Patent Tong Committee

For the purpose of requiring the Department of Natural Resources to have licensed oystermen of this State select a committee composed of a specific number of oystermen who earn their livelihood by catching oysters using diving apparatus; SUPPORT. Governor signed into law.

HB 1052—Striped Bass or Rockfish and Yellow Perch—Comprehensive Management Plan

For the purpose of requiring the Department of Natural Resources to prepare a comprehensive management plan for the harvesting of striped bass or rockfish and yellow perch; requiring the comprehensive management plan General Assembly; SUPPORT. Governor signed into law.

HB 1117—Oyster Shells—Returning to Chesapeake Bay or Tributaries

For the purpose of requiring a commercial oyster packer to reserve for a certain period of time oyster shells for the Department of Natural Resources to have the shells returned to the Chesapeake Bay; providing for a certain right of the State to purchase a certain amount of oyster shells taken from certain State waters; providing for the taking of oyster shells out of the State; providing for notice to and payments of holders of oyster shells taken out of the State; requiring the Department to determine a fair market value for fresh oyster shells. SUPPORT. Governor signed into law.

HB 1191—Anne Arundel County—Crab Pots—Prohibition

For the purpose of prohibiting a person from catching crabs for commercial purposes with a crab pot in certain waters of the Patapsco River in Anne Arundel County; and prohibiting the Department of Natural Resources from adopting regulations contrary to this Act. OPPOSE because it limits harvesting territory. Bill died in Committee.

HB 1301—Aquaculture Operations—Striped Bass—Hybrids

For the purpose of eliminating certain prohibitions relating to hybrids of striped bass or rockfish; prohibiting a person from selling hybrids of striped bass or rockfish at certain times; declaring a hybrid of the species of fish known as striped bass or rockfish not to be a threatened or endangered species for certain purposes; allowing a person to propagate, grow, possess, sell, and transport hybrids of striped bass or rockfish; and generally relating to the propagation, growth, possession, sale, and transportation of hybrids of striped bass or rockfish. SUP-PORT. Bill died in Committee.

HB 1363—Boat Excise Tax—Commercial Watermen

For the purpose of allowing a credit against the boat excise tax on certain vessels for sales tax paid by certain persons on materials and equipment incorporated into the vessels; exempting from the boat excise tax, possession within the State of certain vessels under certain circumstances; prohibiting the Department of Natural Resources from collecting or enforcing the Maryland use tax for certain vessels owned by certain persons; and generally relating to the boat excise tax. SUPPORT. Governor signed into law.

—Plus about 25 other pieces of legislation that must be tackled continuously throughout the legislative process.

Aquaculture and the Bay

The issue of aquaculture and leasing Bay bottomland was one of the major issues for watermen in the legislature. While scientists, environmentalists, and some users and consumers push for the expansion of the aquaculture concept, watermen are fearful that this approach to "farming seafood" will affect them dramatically.

Over 200 watermen, fearful that their livelihoods would be lost, packed the House Environmental Matters Committee hearing room to oppose a state plan to allow commercial farming of fish and oysters (HB-748). The watermen were particularly concerned about a provision that would allow the state to establish aquaculture enterprise zones in the Chesapeake and her tributaries. The state could then lease parcels inside such zones to private businesses interested in laying down oyster beds or launching "fish farm" operations.

"But watermen *depend* on such 'barren bottom' waters," said Larry Simns. "We're going to lose valuable bottom that we use for clamming and crabbing and oysters," he added.

Simns predicted the aquaculture industry would eventually seek an end to restrictions that limit such leases to 100 acres per person. That would enable the industry to monopolize the waters, hurting watermen.

He also criticized another provision that would slap stiff penalties on watermen caught stealing from oyster beds owned by others. Among other sanctions, the bill would strip a violator's fishing license for two years.

"The problem with that is we got a lot of imaginary lines out there," said Simns. He said the bill "goes too fast, too furious" and said the measure is "going to affect too many people's lives to rush into this leasing thing."

"I can't understand for the life of me if this bill was even proofread," said Delegate Richard F. Colburn, D-Dorchester, who pointed out what he considered mistakes in the bill.

Bill Woodfield, owner of a Galesville fish and oyster company and a member of a committee that made recommendations on the bill, said it was hastily drafted, but it was a good start toward getting Maryland into the aquaculture business.

"It's got a lot of flaws. It's got a lot of good things about it," he said.

David Carroll, Governor Schaefer's aide on Chesapeake Bay issues, urged the committee to work with the administration and watermen to write an acceptable bill. He said aquaculture could add a major new component to Maryland's economy.

Secretary of Agriculture Wayne A. Cawley Jr., whose department would be designated the lead agency for the management of aquaculture, argued that fish farming represents hope for both agriculture and the seafood industry, both suffering from serious economic troubles. "The time is right for a new industry in this period of economic change," Cawley said.

Other officials testified that other states are entering the business and Maryland could lose an opportunity if it doesn't allow aquaculture.

Cawley's optimism about aquaculture's future is shared by many in this country and abroad, said Bill Hobart, director of aquaculture for the U.S. Department of Agriculture. He noted that in the mid-1960s, some 2 billion pounds of seafood were produced by aquaculturists worldwide. By the mid-1980s, production had risen to 25 billion pounds. A similar growth pattern has developed in the U.S. In 1970, 130 million pounds were produced in this country, rising to 600 million pounds in 1985.

"It's clear this is a major trend," Hobart said.

The United States imports 64 percent of its seafood now, and increased production from aquaculture would reduce the imports.

"We eat more fish and we have less of it (that) we produce domestically," he concluded.

It will be a long session. Larry and his fellow watermen must also clam and oyster to earn a living while following, testifying, and lobbying on this legislation. And, they are very concerned that they don't have the votes on some important issues.

The Expo

On Friday, January 22, James and I left Annapolis to attend the Maryland Watermen's Association's East Coast Commercial Fisherman's Trade Exposition at the Ocean City, Maryland Convention Hall. The Expo is an annual event attracting watermen and boating enthusiasts from the mid-Atlantic region. It is the Watermen's Association's major fundraiser of the year.

There will be boats on display as well as a wide array of commercial products ranging from paint for crab pots to fish-finding sonar devices. There will also be a Ford truck raffled off on the last day of the show. I bought a ticket, so I have a hidden agenda!

It's Saturday morning and the MWA is holding its Annual Business Meeting. I am greeted at the meeting by Betty Duty and Bill Sieling, head of Maryland's Seafood Marketing Division in the Department of Agriculture. Several watermen, including Louis Cantler from Annapolis, are talking about oysters and crabs before the meeting starts.

"Oysters are all but gone now," Cantler says matter-of-factly. "Men are already workin' on crab pots. The tongers are only gettin' four to six bushels a day at most and the skipjacks are down to 50. Next year, most won't even go out. Everybody will be crabbin' this summer and the number of pots is gonna get worse. The clammers will have to get prop guards."

"Got that right," Larry Simns interjects.

Cantler takes a moment to jibe at Larry about his new boat DAWN II. "I want a boat that will draw six inches, not like your new boat. Hell, you'll run aground in the middle of the Bay!"

"You got that right," Larry smiles again.

"We'll all be wavin' at ya when we go by to the clam beds."

"Yea," Larry says, "and at $100,000 she draws too much money too!" They chuckle as Larry calls the meeting to order.

Comments by Larry are taken in silence and without emotion. Each man in the room, and several wives, listen intently to his remarks. He is emphatic about all disciplines in the industry working together during "hard times" and that the watermen must try and get along with each other, residents, environmentalists, marina owners, and government bureaucrats. "They will kill us if we try to take on the recreational boaters and marinas. We are a minority even when we stick together if we look at how many people are using and moving to the Bay. The Association is representing the big issues, but you all have to put your little skirmishes aside or we'll lose the war. The idea is survival as watermen. We can't keep fightin' amongst ourselves or we'll keep losing," he said.

"Now this year's meetin' is a good first step—we're joining with the packers and the Seafood Industries Association, and that's good. So now the Divers Association, Patent Tong Association, hand tongers, and dredgers need to work together." I notice the oystermen in the room take this suggestion with understanding and, perhaps, reluctance. They know the best approach to the issues facing them is to be united, but their built-in chemistry leads to independence and self-reliance. It is difficult for them to face the reality of the season.

As Larry introduces men from around the state, he concludes by introducing me. "Mick is from the marina/recreational boating sector and he's workin' real close with us and helpin' on the excise tax bill that's against watermen. We think we'll be able to win this and he's testified with us in committee. Thanks, Mick for all your help." His strategy for the weekend would be to subtly remind all these watermen that a different approach to issues is required. They must start working with "outsiders."

I am reminded that there are "outsiders" who do want to work with the watermen. And they are people the watermen can trust. Dr. Rita Caldwell of the University of Maryland Sea Grant Program is a brilliant scientist and a strong supporter. She says, "The watermen have been telling the educational, scientific, and government communities for years what is happening out there on the Bay. We haven't been listening. Watermen are very shrewd observers and very aware. They told us about the dissolved oxygen problem and MSX, originally. Not in those terms exactly, but it was the watermen who brought it to the attention of our community. Sea Grant and other constituencies must become advocates of the watermen." I am hopeful that this woman will be a leader in bringing these groups together.

Larry breezes over a quick status report mentioning that the Government Oyster White Paper Committee—1987 represents the first time the Department of Natural Resources listened to watermen. There was no more dictating by the DNR; on the Striped Bass White Paper Committee, management recommendations are supposed to be presented in July, 1988. There are several bills in the Maryland General Assembly and Larry wants to make sure the fishery is not opened up "without laws to protect watermen and keep a gold rush from happening when they open;" on aquaculture and mariculture he points a finger as the biggest issue of 1988: "Legislation in that would increase leasing dramatically from Delegate Slade. You men from St. Mary's County have to work on him, it's a terrible bill. If it goes through, then I want an amendment that any lease owner caught taking harvest from public rock or oyster beds will lose his leased bottom!" The sarcasm hits home. He wants a survey of Bay bottoms to tell what kinds of bottoms are left and where they are, to see which will yield productive growth. Most watermen will respect leased bottom, but they are concerned that some might get arrested for harvesting on leased bottom that is poorly marked or designated. I recall the three sticks in Mill Creek that Larry pointed out to me while we were clamming. Larry concludes by saying the Slade bill as originally written could put independent watermen out of business.

Fighting for Their Rights

The watermen have major issues with the ISSC and their oyster bed closure policies. The MWA might retain a lawyer to sue the federal government on these issues. Larry mentions that the DNR has announced that catching yellow perch has been closed off in certain areas around the Bay. "It's another instance," he says, "of closing an area instead of fighting the problem. The problem is pollution, especially in the Nanticoke River and the Upper Bay. Pollution is causing closing and they're not fixing pollution. Nanticoke is a small river, they should find out what the problem is, not close the hatchery. A big river like the Hudson has plenty of pollution and still has a huge fish hatchery. So, the government is all backwards again."

A St. Mary's County waterman says that they can produce plenty of seed oyster or spat, but raising them beyond 1 to 1½ inches is impossible because they're dying off. He would like to see an expansion of the seed area in his county and then ship the seed to better growth areas. The only issue there is the long haul from St. Mary's all the way up the Bay. When the men start moving seed oysters the first of March under the state program, he explains that "it's a rough month to try to make money hauling seed, but better money than outright oystering." Larry Simns will talk to the DNR but is concerned that placement of seed be discussed with state directors. "MSX is caused by too much salinity, but if we put 'em too far up in the headwaters, then fresh water will kill them. If we go too deep they will die from lack of oxygen with bad water."

John Page Williams is a friend and staff member of the Chesapeake Bay Foundation. Over the years, John Page has worked closely with men who make their living on the water. He has tremendous respect for them and he's spent thousands of hours merging their efforts with those of the CBF programs.

"Oystering has always been the Bay's economic anchor in winter, but this year it won't be. Already stressed by a combination of environmental problems and harvest pressures, the oyster stocks were devastated last spring by a combination of two parasitic diseases, MSX and Dermo. These diseases pose absolutely no threat to humans, but they have wreaked havoc with the industry. Osyters are scarce; both watermen and seafood packers are having a lean season. This is a good time to look at oyster harvesting techniques as they are currently practiced in the Chesapeake and to think about their future."

It has always been a tradition here that a waterman could pick up a set of tongs, run a workboat (even a skiff in calm waters) out to a public oyster rock (bar), and make a day's work. "The Lord put those oysters here for us," is the popular philosophy.

This is the hunter-gatherer tradition, one of fierce independence and self-reliance, where a man's ability to make a living swings completely on his own hard work and skill at finding oysters. It is prized highly by the people who practice it, often watermen who have learned the craft from fathers, grandfathers, and even great-grandfathers. It is also prized by those of us who are bound to jobs over which we have less control and who derive vicarious satisfaction from the fact that people can still make a living this way.

More Restrictions?

Back in September 1987, for example, the watermen were shocked to find that a committee with no legal or legislative authority could actually force the State of Maryland to close many shellfish beds if an inch of rain fell in a 24-hour period. With the prospects of a poor harvest

due to MSX disease, this possibility of healthy beds being closed en-
raged the watermen.

The new restrictions were established by the Interstate Shellfish
Sanitation Conference (ISSC) and essentially stopped oyster harvests for 3 to 5 days in areas of the Bay where bacteria levels exceeded
national guidelines after an inch of rain.

The new harvest restrictions from the federal commission inspired
the watermen to urge the state government to mount a legal attack on
the ISSC standards. Many of the watermen questioned the authority
of the commission to impose such restrictions. The ISSC is a national
body made up of health officials and representatives of the seafood industry from states that produce or receive seafood. It is not a government agency and cannot make or legally enforce regulations. But the
commission informed Maryland in the spring that its seafood would
be banned from sale in other states if it did not comply with ISSC
standards.

Mary Garreis, of the Maryland Department of the Environment,
said that Maryland decided to comply with the standards set by ISSC
for fear the clam industry would be affected as well as the oyster industry. "Once you get a reputation that your product is questionable," she
said, "then you're going to have trouble selling all your products."

States that have said they would boycott Maryland seafood products include Virginia, Massachusetts, Maine, New Jersey, New York,
North Carolina, Illinois, and Arizona. Garreis said the U.S. Food and
Drug Administration asked that the affected areas be closed to
oystering for five days after an inch of rainfall. The state is holding out
for three. Watermen say that an average rainfall would effectively destroy the oyster season as an economically viable proposition.

Once this position was established by Maryland's bureaucracy, the
Watermen's Association decided to take action themselves. The
group decided to file a federal lawsuit against the ISSC because of the
standards of closure due to rainfall and the imposition of buffer zones
around marinas so that shellfish cannot be harvested in those zones.
The restrictions could influence harvesting in as many as 11 areas of
the Chesapeake region.

Maryland is a member of the Sanitation Conference, a voluntary
organization of 21 shellfish-producing states and 31 shellfish-con-

suming states that has set national standards for shellfish sanitation. As with other issues and outside forces threatening their livelihood, the watermen do not take this federal action lightly.

"This is a case of fixing something that isn't broken, but watermen will be broke if we don't get out from under this, because we can lose most of the oyster season if it rains in the wrong amounts in the wrong times. Clammers will also be affected in some areas," Larry Simns said. "What the ISSC wants is not necessary, because there has never been a problem with Maryland seafood, and that's because our health department has been so good at its job. But, the state has been put in the position of going along with the ISSC because it has threatened our markets. We have been told by the state that they're going to fight this, but if the state doesn't take enough action, we will," Simns said. "We're contemplating a suit."

Simns said that the Food and Drug Administration is using the ISSC standards and the threat against a ban on Maryland seafood in other states "as blackmail. If Maryland caves in, then all the other seafood-producing states will have to cave in, too. Maryland should fight this."

Support for Maryland

In February, the "fight" continued and the Maryland watermen were receiving more than conciliatory support from colleagues in other states.

Two donations, one from Louisiana, bolstered the Maryland Watermen's Association's war chest for legal action against the Interstate Shellfish Sanitation Conference by $1,500, with another $500 pledged.

The Placquemines Oyster Association, responding to the MWA's appeal to watermen's and seafood packers' organizations all over the country, sent a check for $500 and a pledge for $500 more on February 3rd. The Maryland Clammers Association sent a check for $1,000 a week earlier.

"We are deeply concerned about the current situation regarding oyster water monitoring regulations," said John E. Tesvich, president of the Placquemines Oyster Association.

"We are glad that a Louisiana watermen's organization has come to our aid," said Larry Simns. "This shows that Maryland watermen are not alone in opposing these unnecessary restrictions and unrealistic standards." Simns told the group's board of directors in a February 6 meeting, that the ISSC and the U.S. Food and Drug Administration are asking that even more stringent restrictions be applied to shellfish harvesting areas, mostly upriver, which ISSC claims are affected by runoff after rainfall. The new restrictions would impose a five-day closure after an inch of rainfall in a 72-hour period, and would be reopened only after the waters were tested and declared safe. Simns said that the present restrictions, for all practical purposes, mean the loss of a week's work to watermen; the new restrictions could easily double that time.

Joe Sadler, president of the Maryland Clammers Association, said that his group voted to give the MWA money for legal expenses because the ISSC restrictions appear to be a threat to clamming. "Right now the ISSC isn't affecting clamming too much because all the water closed is at the head of creeks, but it looks to us like we have no choice but to fight this thing and support the MWA because it'll affect everybody one way or another in the future," he said.

"Now, a lot of people who don't have market can go oystering, either in a small boat or with somebody else," Sadler said, "and it looks like these people will be hurt. In the end, it'll affect everybody who works on the water."

Simns said that most of the areas affected now by the regulations are not currently shellfish-producing areas, but they could be in the future. But the worst menace, Simns said, is that the ISSC, which can act without holding hearings or observing the rules that restrict the Food and Drug Administration, is doing the federal agency's work for it.

"Last couple of years, what with that pollution an' development, a lot of jobs have been lost on the water. Packing houses for crabs and oysters closing down and the government cut out fishing for Rock. The children don't have jobs so many are forced to leave town for work. There's many a tear been shed by mothers here and all over the Bay I'll tell ya. Fathers, too."

Another Perspective: The DNR

Pete Jensen is Director of the Fisheries Division in the Maryland Department of Natural Resources. He is the man in charge of the watermen's lifeblood, their harvests. Pete Jensen is also the one man in government who the watermen say they "can work with" and they "respect."

On February 8th, I met with Jensen to get a state perspective on the clamming and oyster problems that have prevailed since mid-1987.

"When Massachusetts and Maine placed a stop order on clams, it was not a result of one incident. What people have to understand is there is a very big picture out on the Bay that few of us have really looked at.

"At first there were limited clams. Then, in 1987 there was an abundance of clams and a major downturn in fish and oyster harvesting. Couple that with a moderately good crabbing season for a few men in 1987 and you have men looking at clams for revenue. There were more clams than the market could take, this drove prices down and we had an influx of men without clamming experience coming into the business. The inexperienced clammers were a target for buyers and the men began making deals to try and make money in a soft market. They would throw the clams in a truck and drive them to New England. Their inexperience didn't follow all the regulations on clam protection, so the health departments up north put on an embargo. This sent word out, falsely, that Maryland clams were bad. A whole rumor started because of a few men," he said.

"After that, a few men began catching twice their limit because the clams were there but the prices weren't. Once a few men started doing it, others followed suit. The buyers, knowing this was going on, required the clammers to give them 11 bushels for the price of ten. There was no state enforcement on the over-harvesting, the cheating was not stopped, so it escalated. That was the state's fault, but it added to the domino effect and people had to cheat to make a living.

The third factor adding to a bad situation getting worse was that the oyster disease, and the clam hygiene issues got mixed up, and rumors flew to consumers all over the United States that Maryland seafood was no good. So, we went from a few watermen not properly transporting clams to a national image problem. Watermen, unfortunately, see these individual incidents as hassles rather than the whole scenario and how everything is interrelated. They also don't see themselves as part of the problem," he said.

Jensen never places the blame on one constituency. He is a fair man who appreciates the watermen while protecting the fisheries. "Watermen, the public, and the government all too often think this industry ends at the dock. We must go beyond the dock to look at the packers, buyers, and consumers to develop best management practices," Jensen said.

Jensen knows the economics of the seafood issue. He knows the numbers in the computer runs on harvests and he knows the watermen. "They think they can suffer through hard times. It's their make-up. Their history. This time it's different. They can't survive this present set of crises unless they accept change, and the watermen, for the most part, accept change reluctantly. People don't have to buy seafood here. Shipping and freight systems are very efficient now. The restaurants can get seafood from down south or out west . . . even the Orient. Those businesses will do whatever they have to do to get crabmeat, for example. They don't have loyalty to the watermen, they have loyalty to their customers who want crabmeat on the menu!"

"The watermen must unite. They can't afford to be so independent anymore. They must look at forming co-ops . . . to buy, sell, and so on. They agree on concepts like co-ops, but won't do it. It's a symptom of things happening to them; losing dock space which used to be free and now is several thousand dollars, tourists and developers running the price of real estate up and moving into what have been 'closed' watermen's communities. They are struggling against social changes on shore and ecological changes in the Bay," he added.

"Watermen don't look for the same things out of lifestyles that we do. Sure, anyone can be a waterman, get a license and you are one. People come and go in the industry because, for a time when jobs on land were scarce, they turned to the Bay. But there are certain people with a certain ilk . . . the real watermen. They will always be out there at sunup," Jensen surmised.

Jensen said that one of the government's major problems is quite simply relating to the watermen. "We've done at least two things wrong: first, not heeding a lot of their advice about what was really happening in the Bay ecosystem over the years, and second, being inconsistent about how we enforce the law. We don't need to enforce the law to the letter; most of the time an officer can use compromise and know that there is some leeway. When we don't respond in this fashion, there is friction between the watermen and the marine police. This, too, is a symptom. You see, we in government, citizen activist groups, the marine industry, watermen, and environmentalists really have been putting bandaids on surgical wounds. Everyone means well, but they aren't helping the big picture. We see changes, a lot of them bad on the water, and we respond out of frustration for solutions. But, until everyone in the watershed works together, we really won't have effective management plans, implementation, and enforcement," he concluded.

The buy boat Halfshell waits at Knapps Narrows, Tilghman Island, for the oyster seed replenishment program to begin. Notice the gates forward of the cabin built to hold over 650 bushels of shell on board.

Tonging can be dangerous as many men work on the topsides of their boats, tonging and walking, tonging and walking.

The patent tong rake-like teeth are ready to dive and grab a load of oysters sitting on the river bottom.

There is silence, no engines, only nature at its best.

Hand tonging for oysters on the Choptank River; from the tong to the culling board to select legal-size oysters over 3".

An oyster buy boat off Greenberry Point, Annapolis, takes bushels from the patent tong boat Whipporwill.

Captain Hathoway of Pa's Pride reflects on a day of tonging.

"Watermen are proud. Most would rather starve then go on welfare or government unemployment help. You know you can make more on unemployment than you can puttin' in 12 hours workin' on the water some days and you still find those boys on the boats before sunrise, hopin' for market and a full day's work."

chapter 4

mid-winter update

Gloom Pervades

By mid-February, oyster tongers still put out from such ports as Bellevue, Kent Narrows, Tilghman, and Cambridge Creek on Maryland's Eastern Shore, but catches were slim and prices low for what few oysters the watermen could find. Last week, for example, I spent the day in Solomons Island and a tonger putting in nine hours alone on his workboat only netted six bushels. Many of the men have quit to go ashore for other work, fix crab pots, or simply wait for better times. "I can't make it on $16-a-bushel oysters," said Ralph Lee of Queen Anne's County, a veteran hand tonger who added that this past year's oyster situation is the worst he's ever seen. MSX and Dermo have now reached into areas never affected before and are taking a heavy toll.

An abbreviated view of the situation the first week of February comes from MWA's Joe Valliant, who has been keeping close watch on the situation.

"The Upper Choptank River is probably the most productive area of Maryland's oystering waters these days. The catches are nothing spectacular, but a long day's work will produce a harvest of 8 to 12 bushels a man. Most of the skipjack fleet still working has concentrated on the Choptank below the Bridge, but they work only Mondays and Tuesdays, when they can dredge under power.

On February 5, a day when there was a fair breeze, six Somerset County skipjacks lay tied up in Cambridge Creek, idle and far from home on a good sailing day.

In good weather, a scattering of Eastern Shore patent tongers can be seen working off Annapolis. A few more are still working off Rock Hall, farther up the Bay, and some are working out of Tilghman, but their catches are also small. The waterfront at Crisfield is "dead;" Tilghman Creek and Cambridge Creek are the same. Only the harbors where clammers are concentrated show near-normal activity. Bellevue's little marina is crowded, despite the fact that it ices rather quickly. Boats from Queen Anne's County have joined Talbot boats in the search for the Tred Avon River's scanty oyster crop.

Much of the oyster harvest these days is being gleaned from the edge of tidewater and from far up the tributaries. Many tongers are working out of skiffs with nippers, or picking up oysters by hand at low tide. The catches are small, but they're keeping many a waterman's family going at a time when they have few other resources," Valliant reported.

Maryland's watermen have little room left to maneuver. In times past they could switch fisheries, but nowadays all other fisheries operating at this time of year are either crowded or low-producing.

The winter is the heart of the oyster season but the slack season for soft-shell clamming, however, "There's more getting in clamming every day," said Eddie Walters, a veteran Queen Anne's County clammer. "I see new boats all the time, and that's not good for anybody. But people have got to do something." On February 7, Walters said that he has had market three or four days a week and orders ranging from 8 to 12 bushels. "I could catch my limit every day," he said. "I don't see as many young clams now as I did last year, but last year was exceptional. Every young clam that got big enough to see must have made it to market size."

Most clammers are working on two- and three-day schedules, and the buyers will take less than the daily 15-bushel limit allowed by law.

The price, $25 a bushel, holding doesn't help either, and clammers are worried that it will fall.

David Cantler, another Kent Island clammer, is discouraged. "Clamming's terrible. The market went from four and six days in October to three and four later in the fall, then down to two. I sold clams every day right through the ice, but then the market went back to nothing. I don't look for clamming to be good again until July," he said.

In the past, on the days when they don't have market, many clammers join another boat to oyster, but this year that option is closed for most and not very productive for the rest.

Gloom of the oystermen's season pervades Somerset County. "It's all dead down here and it won't be coming back soon," said Fred Maddox, president of the Somerset County Watermen's Association. Maddox speaks from experience; his area was wiped out by the first MSX epidemic of the early 1960's, a disaster that sent Smith Island watermen to court to break the county lines and up the Bay to oyster for many seasons.

This season many Somerset County patent tong boats and skipjacks could be found off Rock Hall and Annapolis until the catches grew too slim to make working that far away from home profitable. A number of Somerset men have joined the crab dredging fleet down in Virginia; many others are ashore, waiting until crab potting season begins and doing what they can to pay their bills in the meantime.

Lee Wilson, a Crisfield waterman who is crab dredging in Virginia, described the mood around town as "not too optimistic. The oyster business here is dead, everyone's looking forward to crabbing. This is the first time in ten or twelve years there's been no oyster industry here. Things don't seem to be too good in the winter crab business either. Some of the houses that usually pick crabs have stopped," Wilson said.

Although it goes hard against their grain, some watermen in Maryland are being forced to consider state and aid programs to carry them through the slack season. Usually, watermen earn enough over the summer and fall to get through the late winter and early spring, but the profits from what generally is considered to have been a good crab season have long been eaten up by the lean oyster season.

Mostly it's the younger watermen who have been hit hardest financially. Relatively good years of adequate crab and oyster catches and high prices encouraged them to undertake heavy debt loads for homes, boats, and vehicles. "The younger guys are having it rough," said Larry Simns. "They didn't know how bad things could get; they haven't lived through enough bad times to be cautious about money." But, as Simns pointed out, no one three years ago could have predicted that Maryland's oyster harvest would be cut in half. The MWA is lobbying hard for help in the form of short-term loans, and DNR has lead an interagency task force to seek other financial help. But watermen simply don't qualify for most aid programs. "Seems like there's no help available if you don't need it all the time," said one angry waterman. "If you've got anything at all, you can't get nothing from the state 'till it's all gone."

Simns Speaks

On March 16, Larry Simns addressed the Annual Marine Trades Association Conference in Annapolis, Maryland. Over 150 recreational boating business owners and managers were in attendance. Simns' assignment was to address the marina owners and developers, yacht sales personnel, and others.

"We are all Bay users, and with waterfront access and development increasing, the number of boats increase. Watermen are coming off a poor oyster harvest and will really have to make up their losses in crabbing. Our men have to use the Bay to make a living, and your customers use the Bay to relax and recreate. We as the main organizations must work together on common issues," he said.

Simns pointed out that two major threats to the watermen's way of life were residential condominium development and poor sewage treatment facilities.

"Developers come into an area and find a shucking (oyster) house that is temporarily out of business in hard times. They offer the owner a big pile of money and he sells. The developers bulldoze the packing or shucking house to build residences and a marina. Where that leaves us when the Bay comes back in three or four years is commercial men with one less place to sell their catch and no place to tie up their boats. The new development has taken them away forever, and you can't really have packing or shuckin' houses back off the water because of access for us, and residences have zoning restrictions against them. We lose badly.

"The next problem is sewage treatment plants because the state of the art now lags way behind what's needed, and governments aren't putting enough money in to bring them up to do a good job. We see whole areas around the sewage discharge areas that are totally dead. Boats and farms are criticized for polluting the Bay, but I think if we don't do something about treatment plants, the boats and farms won't really matter," he said.

"If we can't produce enough income from oysters and can't harvest striped bass, then we have to turn to crabs. Now crab pots are a big issue with boaters, but the boaters have to learn to stay clear of the buoys. Boaters like to take the shortest and fastest route somewhere, and it strikes me funny because they're supposed to be out relaxin'," Simns says as his comment draws laughter from the boating business owners.

"If a crabber lays out 800 to 900 pots this season at about $15 each, by the end of the season he'll lose 400 to recreational boat props and weather. He can't afford the loss and your people can't afford the potential damage to a shaft or propeller blade. So we're workin' on a couple of things; one is a re-designed pot which has less visibility through a reduction in vertical height. The other is a brochure that Mick Blackistone wrote to go to all Maryland recreational boaters on using their boats around watermen and their equipment." I was pleased he mentioned my brochure because there were state government employees present at the conference and we would have to use Maryland's Waterway Improvement Fund dollars for printing and distribution of the brochure.

"Now another issue is we have to crab closer and closer to shore because pollution is chasing the crabs to healthier water. If there's no oxygen in the water and we throw pots over the next day, all we get is a pot full of dead crabs and that don't help anybody, so we have to go closer to shore or shoal areas. Residents may complain about the danger of the pots, but their real issue is probably the noise of the boats early in the mornin'. We need to work with everybody because if it's the noise and not the pots themselves, I can call the men workin' in that area and ask them to start their engines later in the mornin' a little bit. A little cooperation might solve some potential problems," Simns said.

Larry Simns discussed these and other issues for about 45 minutes and was well received by the business owners. Each time I hear him speak, I am more intrigued by his vast knowledge and ability to "sell" the attributes of his profession and their relationship with other Bay users.

The watermen are being hit hard in the Maryland General Assembly 1988 session. On numerous occasions during the past two months, I have watched and listened as they presented their case before the House of Delegates or Senate. During Maryland's 90-day legislative session, Simns and his colleagues testified and lobbied on a variety of issues that are in many cases critical to the survival of their industry and livelihood. The men look out of place in the marble halls of the Maryland State House among pinstriped suits, legal pads, and fast-paced politicking. But they are there and they are respected, for the most part, for who they are. I have testified numerous times on maritime issues and each time I prepare written comments. This approach helps me get through the nervousness and assures me that I will make all my points for a convincing argument for or against a piece of legislation. Larry Simns and his colleagues, however, rarely, if ever, use notes or provide anything in writing. They know their issues well and they are single-minded about their agenda. I constantly am impressed.

Losing the CLARENCE CROCKETT

On March 17, as thousands of Marylanders left work early to celebrate St. Patrick's Day festivities with green beer races and leprechaun posters, the Deal Island skipjack CLARENCE CROCKETT sank in the Chesapeake Bay.

Captain Paul Holland, a 40-year-old Deal Island waterman and his two crew members were on their way home from oystering in the upper Chesapeake when the CROCKETT hit a marker and went down. The three men clung to a Wicomico County line marker for 14 hours in Tangier Sound in 20 degree weather waiting to be rescued.

Well aware of the critical danger they faced, the watermen, staved off constant fear with their determination to save themselves. By continually talking to each other they stayed awake; no one would slip from the 2-inch-wide ledge and fall into the choppy water which was cold enough to kill them in minutes. "That was the only thing that kept us alive. We didn't allow anyone to sleep," said Holland.

The 45-foot skipjack was built 80 years ago in Deep Creek, Virginia, and was one of only 22 sailing workboats left in the United States.

The crew eventually was rescued by Natural Resources Police on a routine patrol. Rescuing the boat turned out to be more difficult.

Holland said he needed $6,000 in cash to pay to have the boat raised from 10 feet of water where she lay. After an oyster season that yielded less than 400,000 bushels statewide, the Deal watermen said he "just didn't have the money. I'm overdrawn, and my mortgage is piling up," he added, "I don't know what I'm going to do."

Holland spent $7,000 to put the CROCKETT in shape last fall, but the oyster harvest had been so poor that he had been unable to make enough to pay the first of the bills. I am reminded of remarks by skipjack captains Russell Dize and Robbie Wilson who continually point out the difficulty in coming up with insurance for the boats since the sinking of the PRIDE OF BALTIMORE. The fact remained, however, that this particular 80-year-old legacy to the Bay wouldn't survive long in the water. "High winds and waves will beat her against the bottom and tear her apart," Holland exclaimed. "She's got to be gotten up soon if she's going to be saved," he said.

Irony seemed to be a part of this man's life. He'd just been in Annapolis when the House of Delegates celebrated the release of the U.S. postage stamp celebrating the 200th anniversary of Maryland's ratification of the U.S. Constitution. The stamp was made from a painting of the CLARENCE CROCKETT sailing by Annapolis Harbor.

In the ensuing weeks the CROCKETT was raised and taken to Crockett's boatyard in Crisfield for rehab work. Sympathetic supporters donating time, services, and money will revive the CROCKETT. As with other tragedies or traumatic situations affecting the watermen, the incident for the most part went unnoticed by many citizens in the Bay region. Holland, like his colleagues before him, will struggle to hold onto his livelihood, and he'll be at the mercy of a handful of funding and service organizations and friends who will put the CROCKETT in a priority ranking according to need.

As I thought of the skipjack going down and the fears of the men, I began to imagine the constant fears and thoughts of families left on shore. In this case, I fantasized about Darla Holland and her young son and of what went through her mind:

When the CROCKETT Went Down

We will wait impatiently
        your son and me
searching the harbor
        for your returning lights

You with your aging mistress
        CLARENCE CROCKETT
aim for home, and island refuge,
        safe from choppy seas

The night stays pitch
        your cry falls on deaf ears
As I sense your fears
        and you sense mine

As you cling to life's marker
        and I to our son
we pray in unison
        that the Bay will be
                forgiving.

MSB

A Look Back

With my legislative responsibilities winding down, I decided to call Bill and Jeane Cummings to see if I could visit with them now that the gloomy oyster season is behind. At 62, Bill Cummings has worked on the water for over 48 years. He has made a good living over almost five decades and his "semi-retirement" is occupied with hand tonging on PA's PRIDE, owned by his friend Captain Hathoway. Hathoway's boat was pulled March 30 for maintenance and fiberglass work, so I knew Bill would be around the Island most days and evenings. When I reached Jeane Cummings by telephone I received the usual Tilghman reception of warmth and openness. "You come right over Monday evening. Won't bother us at all and Bill and I will talk as long as you want to," she said. I am still uneasy, after all this time, about intruding into the homes of the watermen, but my reservations generally are cut off sharply by the men and women who work on the water. They are most anxious to make things easy for me and as in the past, I am emphatically told by Mrs. Cummings to "come over for sure. I'm only fixin' a one potter for dinner so won't be a bother and we'll be ready to see you."

On Monday April 4, as I drove onto Tilghman I felt a wave of relief and excitement. Relief because I was away from the hustle of State House activity and excitement because at 6:30 p.m. the men in their pickups were criss-crossing the roadways like an army of ants on a hunt as they prepared for oyster seeding and crabbing. As I approached the bridge connecting North Tilghman with the Island, I saw Captain Robbie Wilson installing plywood frames above the sides of the BRENDA II so that he can begin carrying seed oyster under the state program. Brenda Wilson was on shore talking to another couple. Robbie lived up to his reputation and kept working until dark.

When I arrived at the Cummings home on the main street, "within hollerin' distance of the country store," I was greeted warmly by Captain Cummings.

Bill Cummings is a large, quiet man. As we began to talk, he grew more and more serious. The good-natured joking that breaks up the monotony of working in the quiet solitude of a shaft tong vessel was absent. "I'll tell you what Mick. For the first time in 50 years I'm puzzled about what to think on oysters and the future. It's a hard fact for anybody to imagine what's going on," he sighed.

"The scientists, environmentalists, and university people are having a field day and receiving all this grant money, and the watermen sit and listen to those experts contradict themselves all day long. How can somebody give a scientist a grant to study the death of an oyster for ten years? Don't make sense. I don't think it's the farmers. They work good with us now. For example, oysters are dead on rock (oyster beds) out in the channel, the river or the Bay, but you can go up some of those creeks that are surrounded by farms and you find nice healthy oysters. That tells me the problem can't all be runoff from the farms. They're helping us now but I'll be surprised if the developers or city sewage treatment plants are lookin' out for this water anywhere."

I reflect for a moment that countless meetings have been held with the farm community to develop best management practices over the past decade. Farmers, especially those in Pennsylvania's Susquehanna River Basin, had been criticized for fertilizer or pesticide runoff into the north Bay's fresh water content. With Bill Cummings' analysis in mind, perhaps the farmers are really making contributions and their efforts are having a positive impact on clam and oyster beds in certain areas.

As the front door opens, Jeane Cummings appears with a gregarious "Hello there, Mick," and quickly displays a bag of fresh kale with pride. After a quick trip to the kitchen she returns to the living room to join us. There are unwritten rules in the watermen's culture including one that I have witnessed where women, for the most part, stay in the background and the men speak of the industry, harvests, and politics. Jeane Cummings violates such codes with outspoken candor. I immediately enjoy talking with her. Her cards are on the table and Captain Cummings laughs periodically at her openness and frank statements. There is love in this room and an unquestionable partnership in life.

"Let me tell you three things," Jeane says, "when some government agency comes to the Tilghman fire hall to sign men up for food stamps, and, Robbie Wilson is sellin' his skipjack, and, you can't believe a word the DNR says, things are bad for the watermen."

Bill is surprised to hear about the food stamp program reaching

Tilghman and emphasizes that, "We don't want no free ride. Watermen want to work. We are very proud people, but if some of these young men have to feed their babies and the hatchery is gone, then maybe some will have to get food stamps. I don't know. It puzzles me," he said.

"All we have in the Bay is a natural resource and the government can take it away from us. This aquaculture or leasing bottom program the governor is pushing in the General Assembly will take the Bay from us. If they do aquaculture inland that's okay, but if they do it overboard (in the Bay) I'm against it," he said.

"People, even recreational boaters, don't understand what will happen if this lease law goes through. Some big company will lease bottoms and actually stake it out so you can't run a boat over it. That's what it will come to."

I emphasize that Governor Schaefer and his administration seem to be an encouragement to the watermen and look for a response.

"Now, I thought he would be all right. He was a great mayor for Baltimore. But, when he pushes the leasing law, I'm against him and it. So much of politics is lip service. And the proof comes out when we look at the law books and regulations.

"I started goin' to the State House when I was 12 years old with my father. He would talk about two big issues for watermen: rockfish and leasing. Here we are 50 years later and I'm going to the State House to talk about the same thing," he said.

"The problem today, though, is the fishery is gone and we may end up with leasing. See, it used to be that some of the men fished while others clammed or oystered. Now all we have is crabs and clams, so everybody jumps in there. That will hurt those harvests. Why, we used to have 20 to 25 pound nets off Tilghman, today there's not a one. I would leave here in March and go up to the Northern Bay. We'd stay from March through June fishin' herring and shad. We had a packing house right in Havre de Grace. Now there's no herring and no shad. Over-fishing didn't kill those industries, the spawn wasn't there. I don't know why."

Mrs. Cummings interrupts by saying, "Oysters is another example; a man shaft tonging might get three or four bushels a day, now, and I've seen a time when Bill would catch 64 bushels in a day by himself."

Bill interjects that patent tongers may be averaging 8 to 10 bushels a day, but running two engines is expensive.

"The young men have to get involved in the legislative process. We have to pull together or we could lose everything we got . . . or what little's left. Larry Simns does a fine job but needs more support from men all over the state," Bill concedes.

He explains that a sad reality is the young watermen "don't know what they've missed because they've never had the great years. I'm talkin' about men under 30 years old."

Like other older watermen, Cummings is concerned that young people on the water aren't planning for the future with IRAs or education and have their mind set that if they make $200 on Monday, they'll make $200 the next day and the next. "They don't stop to think that the next Saturday they may only make $10 because of a blow or rain, but they don't plan for that setback," he says. Some of these boys love the independence of the water and the instant money on good days so much they don't realize the fishery is actually gone . . . partly because the young ones never had it."

"I made workin' on the water very undesirable for my boys and neither one got into it. My grandson wanted to be a waterman, bought his crab pots, has a boat and at 21 will work to make it. He seems pretty determined, even workin' Sundays but me and Jeane are worried to death about him."

Jeane steps in and says she remembers vacations in Mexico and having $500 to go shopping in Easton. "It was a real good life for us, but in the last eight years we haven't hardly had a day off. At least, no vacations to speak of and the future don't look any better."

Captain Bill Cummings continually drifts back to the aquaculture/ leasing bottoms issue. "I'll tell you what infuriates me. The governor goes to Japan and see how aquaculture works and somebody says if the Japanese had the Chesapeake Bay, they could feed the world! Well, let me tell them that our watermen could feed the world if the Bay was right. But it's not. And you can't compare the Chesapeake to the Sea of Japan, the Gulf of Mexico or any of those tropical water areas. We have cold water six months and warm water the next. In our water it takes an oyster three years to grow. In tropical water it's a lot shorter period of time. Big differences, but these legislators are being made to believe it's the same principle."

I am amazed at the depth of concern this experienced waterman has over this single legislative issue, an issue that has been with him since he visited Annapolis with his father 50 years ago. His occasional optimism that nature might be able to turn around the oyster devastation and restore the harvest potential and the fisheries is subtle but forthright. He has tremendous faith and a hope that he will be proven wrong when he says "the future doesn't look very bright and we may be seeing the end of a way of life in the Chesapeake."

While Bill Cummings recognizes that the present way of life for the Maryland watermen and their families is changing, though he is just over 60 years old, the way of life he was born into has been gone for more than 15 years.

"There was a time when Tilghman Island and Rock Hall were the biggest commercial fishing places in Maryland," he said. "There were 25 or 30 fishermen working out of Tilghman 'til the early 1960's, and they employed about 50 men. Now there are none, and all those jobs are gone," Cummings said.

Long before the Department of Natural Resources placed a moratorium on the catching of striped bass, most Tilghman Islanders abandoned the demanding life of the commercial netter. First, the herring and shad disappeared, then the striped bass, and the fisherman, caught in a tangle of increasingly restrictive regulations, reluctantly abandoned the fishery.

Bill Cummings loved fishing; he'd be fishing today if he could, instead of changing from oyster tonging to crabbing as he was the first week of April.

"I always fished," he said. "When I was a young man, nobody crabbed much. Crabbing was a last resort, something you did when you couldn't make money any other way."

But fishing is still alive in Bill Cummings' memory, and he uses the talent he was born with and the skill he's developed over the years to record these memories with pen and paintbrush.

Moments later I realize that the lifelike painting on the wall over the television bears the artist's inscription "William Cummings." "Is that yours? You painted that?" I asked with obvious excitement.

"Yea, that's one of mine," he said proudly and shyly. It turns out that Cummings is Tilghman's own artist. Working in a back room of his house, he turns out paintings and drawings of watermen at work. Most of his art concentrates on fishermen, and it's clear that Bill Cummings knows his subject firsthand. There's power in a painting of men hauling a seine (small fish) ashore. Looking at it and listening to the artist talk about what the painting shows is the next best thing to being there, and it seems certain now that looking at pictures of haul seining will be the closest the younger generation will come to that ancient method of fishing.

"I've been fooling with drawing ever since I was a kid," he said, but his wife claims credit for steering him to painting. She bought him some artist's canvas she found on a Christmas-time expedition to Baltimore in 1948. Cummings sells his work, so consequently he has little of it on display in his home.

"There's a lot of history in these pictures," he said. "You can't get a picture of what's in these paintings with a camera, it isn't there anymore."

Over the years, he's turned out hundreds of paintings for sale, "three-quarters of them pertaining to the water business."

"I was born on Kent Island," Cummings said, "but my father was from Tilghman Island, and he soon moved us back. My father and grandfather were watermen. I guess we've been watermen as far back as anyone can remember.

"I started working with my father when I was a boy—haul seining. I worked with him until 1948, when I had Maynard Lowrey build a boat for me. I call her ZACA, which means peace of mind, and I still have her. We're going down together."

Asked about close calls on the water, Cummings grinned. "I've had several. As an old man you look back on what you did when you were a young man, and it scares you.

"Before we had radios, a breakdown in the wintertime could be disastrous. There was no communication with the shore at all, but watermen would always try to find you.

"We fished in the worst season of the year, and when it was blowing and freezing at the same time, you were in a dangerous situation. You had to keep running, and you had to keep the ice off the boat whatever else you did."

The physical side of net fishing was hard, even in the best weather, Cummings recalled, and he showed hands scarred by net cuts and by splitting open from too much contact with cold air and water. He showed powerful hands with long fingers distorted by the labor of years of net handling and recalled the sting of salt in open cuts, and, worse, the kerosene used to preserve cotton nets. "It was better when we got linen netting, and then nylon," he said.

But rough as commercial fishing was, Bill Cummings never wanted to do anything else. Long before he was of voting age, he was a professional waterman.

"When I was 14, I wanted to quit school and go to work full time, but my father wanted me to get an education. So, one day he took me out fishing. It was very cold, and I damn near froze to death, he wouldn't let me get inside the cabin. I told him that if he'd put me ashore, I'd stay in school," Cummings recalled. "I did finish school, but I also wanted to be out on the water every chance I got."

"We could fish summer and winter in those days," he said. "We didn't need much regulation because you couldn't sell a small fish, and we had plenty of fish to catch: shad, herring, croaker, and rockfish.

"In winter we used to meet the Rock Hall boys in Solomons. Everybody gathered there to avoid being frozen in, and we'd work our way up to the head of the Bay through the spring. Everybody got along good together and we kept an eye on each other in bad weather.

"We didn't have much to do in Solomons. There was one movie house, built on a pier, I think it's a restaurant now, and one bar in town. We lived on our boats, and came home most weekends.

Cummings has some very definite ideas about the cause of the decline of commercial fishing. "We didn't overfish," he asserted, "there were too many restrictions on us for that, and they were enforced. Something has happened to the water on the spawning grounds, especially at the head of the Bay, and the government should be finding out what's going on and doing something about it instead of restricting watermen."

First shad and herring disappeared, he recalled, then the striped bass declined. "Even the 'swell' toad are gone," he said.

"Our water hasn't been right since Hurricane Hazel (1954)," Cummings said. "Scientists can put a name and number on things, but they still haven't shown me anything because they haven't fixed what's wrong."

Cummings has seen a great many changes in the way watermen work, and most of them involve things that once were plentiful, but have disappeared. The decline of commercial fishing means that a whole variety of gear once common in Maryland is gone, or very scarce.

Boats are bigger and more powerful nowadays, he said, but the most important change in their equipment involves marine electronics. "When radios first came into use, we thought that was something wonderful," he said, "because when you broke down alone out there, you really were on your own, and that's a bad feeling.

"Now they've even got radar and Loran so they can go where they want to unless there is ice or a bad storm."

But the most important and significant change Bill Cummings has seen involves changes in the water quality.

"When I was a young man, I never saw the red water, or crabs dying in the pot, or how they run from red water. Then our grasses disappeared.

"They (DNR officials) talk about saving the 1982 year class of rock-fish with this ban, but they're not doing any good so long as the water is bad and they can't spawn. Bad water will be the end of them, and I'd hate to see that.

"I've seen the fish spawning at the head of the Bay, big rock rolling on their sides and spawning—the shad and herring too. It was a beautiful sight."

Nowadays Cummings oysters and crabs, "much to my sorrow. It makes me sick when I think what's happened to us," he said. "I've hopes that I'll see the Bay come back the way it was, but I don't think it'll be soon.

"I have only been trotlining several years—I crab potted for 15 years, and in 1985 I tried eeling for the first time. I only lasted two weeks at it, and they were the two most miserable weeks I spent in my life.

"I'd love to see the Bay come back, but I don't think all this publicity about pollution is going to help the watermen any. People don't understand, they think the seafood is polluted and they're afraid to eat it."

But, while Cummings mourns the end of commercial fishing as he knew it, he celebrates it with his art. "I've got a lot of calls for my pictures," he said, "and I'm glad of that, but what I'm painting is history, and that's a real shame."

By 10:00 p.m. Bill, Jeane, and I are feeling weary and I feel that I'm pushing on my welcome; they don't, but I prepare to leave anyway. I am left with a warning to watch for deer crossing the road between Tilghman and St. Michaels, a 16-mile trip where I pass only one other driver in the dead of night. The deer would be safe crossing the road here.

Captain Hathoway.

The boats, shantys, and men of Smith Island have been with the grand dame Chesapeake throughout time. Some wonder how long the relationship will last.

Patent tong rigs from as far south as Smith Island spent weeks during the winter in Annapolis waters searching for oysters unaffected by MSX or Dermo disease.

A crabbing skiff won't be used for work today—the whole family leaves for a ride.

Skipjack races at Chesapeake Appreciation Days, 1987, Annapolis, a day of fun drawing attention to the watermen and their vessels.

"I'd say we ain't like farmers. We're the closest thing to the Indians. See, the white man came and took a little of this and a little of that until the Indians didn't have nothin' left. There's still some Indians that cling to the old ways but not many. Watermen are a lot like that with outsiders takin' a little bit of this and a little bit of that with the developments and population, and we still cling to our ways. It's the quality of life . . . not the money."

chapter 5

spring

A Time to Replenish

With spring upon the Chesapeake, reflection on the close of the oyster season 1987 to 1988 is met with trepidation and reserve. The harvest would cull out at approximately 350,000 bushels, less than half of the 1986 season. From one end of the Chesapeake Bay to the other, dialogue among the men is often the same . . . "we just scraped by" or "we worked in the hole all season."

The watermen have faced hard times before but it seems that more are seeking other economic alternatives this year than in the past. George O'Donnell, a young Queen Anne's County oyster diver, and a strong advocate of watermen's issues and programs didn't go diving for oysters in the fall. Instead, harvest and the economic outlook led him to Washington D.C. to work for a construction company building bridges. There are many George O'Donnells in the waterfront communities.

For the first time in a long, long while the price of oysters this winter didn't rise to compensate for lack of harvest . . . they did rise enough, however, to close the doors of several Maryland and Virginia packing houses whose owners could not afford to shuck the Maryland oysters or live off dollars generated by oysters bought from out-of-state sources.

It wasn't long ago, for example, that Harris Seafood on Kent Island was shucking 800 to 1,000 bushels of oysters a day. This season, only 40 bushels were shucked on a good day and good days averaged only twice a week, according to Jerry Harris, president of the company.

In the southern Chesapeake on Smith Island, a community held together through generations by the bounty of the bay's seafood industry, perhaps more than any other community in Maryland, watermen hung on to the barren season oystering far from home. Other men switched to crab dredging in late 1987 and by January, most were staying at home making ready for crabbing.

The historic skipjack oyster fleets of Tilghman and Deal Islands are a dying legacy and doubts have arisen about the future of America's last working sailing fleet. "For Sale" signs have appeared on skipjacks even prior to the last snow melt and crews often didn't show up for work because the money "just couldn't be made."

"I've been dredging for 40 years, and this is the worst season I've ever seen," said Captain Peter Sweitzer, of the skipjack HILDA WILL-ING. "I suspect a lot of skipjacks will go out of business this year. There are a few, maybe ten, that can survive."

Hand tonging, the oldest and most tradition bound method of catching oysters did the best I suppose—if they had markets. Near the end of the season, they didn't have them either.

And so aside from the economic and emotional havoc wrought on watermen and their families by plain hard times, the MSX and Dermo disease outbreaks and extensive government regulation, the entire image of Maryland's seafood industry was hurt by the media and their stories on disease-laden seafood.

As mentioned throughout this book, watermen are die-hard fighters for their way of life. Even when they have been set back, they have unshakeable faith. Many watermen took up clamming and net fishing in the colder months and began to eel and crab almost a month earlier this year over last.

Ralph Lee, president of the Queen Anne's County Watermen's Protective Association and son of a life-long waterman, harvested oysters for only two weeks in November. He made more reliable money painting this winter.

The 1988 oyster replenishment program allows the watermen to make some money and plant enough seed oyster to lay some optimism in the future.

This year's repletion program had a double objective: to plant as much seed as possible far up the Bay and the tributaries where MSX and Dermo are less of a threat, and to put down as much shell as possible on seed and natural bars to build them up.

"We've agreed the salvation of the oyster industry statewide is seed," W. Peter Jensen, the DNR's tidal fisheries director, told Eastern Shore legislators on April 1.

This year's replenishment program is the most ambitious ever undertaken. On April 4, watermen and the DNR began planting seed— about 713,500 bushels. Jensen said that some $600,000 has been allocated to move seed, if there's enough seed to move. Nine counties will get shares of the approximately 200,000 bushels of fresh shells DNR has been able to purchase from packing houses.

Later in this spring 5.8 million bushels of dredged shells will be planted at carefully selected locations around the Maryland portion of the Chesapeake Bay. Approximately 2.2 million bushels will go to state seed areas, 835,000 bushels on sanctuaries, 2 million on "seed-and-leave" areas where mortality risk is thought to be acceptable, and 560,000 bushels will be used to build up natural oyster bars.

To make working in the seed (shell) program more attractive to watermen, the DNR this year adjusted its pay rates. Watermen who haul seed on runs up to five miles will receive 75 cents a bushel, runs of five to thirty miles will pay 97 cents and runs over thirty miles will pay $1.08. We think the short-range price is equitable, and we've reduced the mileage and raised the price to more fairly compensate the long runs," Jensen said. "There won't be many short runs this year, I'm afraid."

While watermen get paid to plant the seed and shell, according to Jensen, the number who participate in the program rarely varies with the quality of the season. So even though this year was the worst on record, he doesn't expect more than the number who planted seed and shell last year—about 200—to do it this year.

"Some of them chose simply not to do it, because they don't want to beat their equipment to death," Jensen stated. In a good day, one boat can make about $165 hauling seed, he said.

The Seafood Packing Industry: Hard Times

In April, the Annapolis "Capital" followed the legislative session with this account of the seafood packing industry. I thought it worth reproduction:

"Nagging questions invade Jerry Harris' mind as he gazes out of the second-story office building of W. H. Harris Seafood Inc. of Kent Island.

Should he build a restaurant? Or maybe office buildings or condominiums? What about a marina?

The boat pulling up to the packing plant's dock below brings him back to the harsh reality of the present, the watermen may have a few oysters, but not enough to bother hiring shuckers.

"We've had an architect draw up plans for a large restaurant," Harris said. "I know we're sitting here on a valuable piece of property and you don't have to have packing plants right on the water."

Harris also has considered other options for the site where his family's seafood packing plant has stood for 41 years.

It is a sign of the times for what was once a thriving business along the shores of the Chesapeake Bay and its tributaries. The ravages of nature and abuses of man have nearly destroyed the Bay's once-bountiful harvest. Signs of life and possible solutions are coming slowly, too slowly for some.

This year, 100-year-old McNasby's was forced to close despite an infusion of money and new technology from a group of three investors who had hoped to save the Eastport establishment.

"It's a sad story," said Jerome J. Parks, an Annapolis developer and one of the partners who tried to save McNasby's.

Harris has managed to survive in part because of a national reputation and the ability to buy oysters from southern states where the growing season is shorter and the oysters healthier. He also handles clams and crabs that for now, are more plentiful.

"You just don't have the product to work with," Harris says. "When you don't have the product you can't compete."

Unlike Harris, George W. Hill Jr. built his business on crabs. But even though Maryland crabs are still plentiful, Hill has to go out of state for crabs during the winter months to keep his regular customers.

On his desk is a quotation from Robert Browning: "A man's reach should exceed his grasp, or what's a heaven for?"

Twenty years ago, Hill was making the daily trek across the Bay Bridge and bringing crabs and clam bait to his co-workers when they asked. The demand got so heavy that he bought a truck and set up business at his Dominion Road home. "It was just me and I stayed in that truck 20 hours a day," he recalled. Hill now has nine trucks, and ships crabs all over the United States. From now until December, there will be about 18 employees at the plant.

Unlike the oyster business, crab houses have grown.

"When I started, there were only about three buyers on the Island. Now we've got about 35 or 40. Most people went for the oysters and oysters look bad," he said.

Hill was among the first and his customers have been loyal. He has expanded his business to the West Coast and Japan. He's also negotiating with companies in West Germany and Poland.

When he retires in three years, Hill's children will continue the business: A daughter already runs daily operations and two grandchildren work during the summer.

"I had some buyer offer me half a million for it last year, but I decided to hold on to it," he said. Hill is confident that his business will continue. Those who depend primarily on oysters face a much more uncertain fate.

When William H. Harris, Jerry Harris' father, started his oyster company in 1947, there were 14 oyster houses at Kent Narrows and a total of 20 in Queen Anne's County. Harris says there were about 70 plants in the state when he started.

Today, there are about a dozen seafood packing plants left, according to Bill Sieling, chief of seafood marketing for the State of Maryland.

"Five years ago there were at least 20. They've been going by the boards for years. It's been a gradual decline," Sieling said. He blames a lack of supply and increased competition from other states for the packing plant decline.

"The southern states and the West Coast can grow oysters and pack them cheaper than we can," Sieling said. "Now, buyers for the large chain stores are buying strictly on price." Maryland's "ace in the hole" had always been the superior oyster. But this year there has been neither quantity nor quality.

Clams, virtually nonexistent two years ago, have come back, but the challenge now is finding a market for them, Sieling said. Skyrocketing land prices have also convinced some packing plant owners that selling the land and reinvesting the money or retiring is a more attractive future than the uncertain seafood market.

The irony is that legislation designed to protect the Bay and help restore its health triggered the upward spiral in land values that makes selling an attractive option.

Yet another problem for the industry is less-than-honest packers who skimp to keep prices down, a practice that Harris and Sieling said affects the entire industry.

"It's hurting us when they do this because we are still giving people a quality product, but people seem to be going after the cheaper product," Harris said. "This has hurt a lot of packers who tried to stay in business."

Sieling compares the seafood business to farming, there are good years and bad, but the good years are enough to carry the business through the bad. But, like the dwindling number of family farms, the seafood packing houses are slowly folding because the good years have not been good enough.

William Harris, who has seen both sides, remains philosophically optimistic. "I have to believe like my father always said, that it will go and it will come. So, I hope someday it will come back," the 66-year-old Harris said. "The clams were bad two years ago. But they came back," he said.

The elder Harris predicted the Bay's decline in 1975 when a reporter from New York interviewed him. "I saw the grasses and everything dying and I knew we would have a dead Bay. We don't have fish, fin fish. The Bay is worse than I ever thought it would be," Harris said recently as he recalled his decade-old prediction.

Harris, who gave up his life on the water for a stint in the service in 1942, started his business five years later after working two years in a general store.

"I put all my effort into this business and for three or four years it was tough," he said.

In the 1950's, Harris started expanding, selling in different parts of the country. From $150,000 in sales the first year, the business grew to $4 million, he said. From 18 employees, the company grew to 75.

"I never wasted money. It was nothing for me to put in 16-hour days. I never took a vacation until 1978," Harris recalled.

Jerry Harris came into the family business 22 years ago. Like his father, he has seen the changes firsthand. Three years ago, Harris closed one of his two oyster shucking plants. Since then, shucking at the remaining plant has dwindled from 1,000 bushels a day to 600 to finally just the overflow.

A bushel of oyster once yielded six to eight pints. In the last two years, that has shrunk to four pints. This year it was only three.

Clams are another story, but Jerry Harris is cautious about what the season will bring. "It seems to be doing all right. But, let's wait until this summer. We'll see . . . ," he said.

Jerry Harris talks calmly about the future and a past when work was a joy.

"I started off working on the water and I wish I'd stay there," he said, his voice a mixture of mild anger tinged with regret and frustration. "But, it's like your mom and dad tell you, that some day this is going to be yours, so you better get in here and learn the business." And now, is he prepared to continue the business and pass it on to his sons? "I honestly don't know," he said. One son spent two years in college, then returned to the water.

"We're looking at a lot of options. I don't think the State wants to see the seafood industry disappear."

Maybe not. But salvaging the industry will take time, creative ideas, money, and desire.

I don't think the State owes anybody an obligation to keep them in business," Sieling said. "But Maryland certainly has done just about anything to keep some businesses. I think the seafood industry is in much the same way."

Out on the Bay Again

On April 18, the alarm went off at 2:59 a.m., and I awoke ironically and reluctantly to "Everybody's Working for the Weekend" by Loverboy. God, these watermen get up early! I'm scheduled to drive southwest of Cambridge to Madison Bay on the lower Eastern Shore. Ronnie Fithian, former president of the Kent County Watermen's Association and resident of Rock Hall, Maryland, will meet me on his boat the MARGARET for a day of seeding oysters. I wanted to see this operation first hand.

The MARGARET is a 57-foot-long wooden boat that Fithian bought three years ago from a fellow on Kent Island for $25,000. She was built in 1912 and is powered by a 671 Detroit Diesel engine. He only uses her for the 3- to 5-week oyster seed program. The rest of the year he keeps her in Rock Hall. He also has a clam boat that he works year 'round.

Since I'm coming from Annapolis, and Ronnie, his mate Jimmy, and his dog Magic are coming from Rock Hall, we agreed to meet in Easton at 5:00 a.m. It will be another 45-minute drive to Madison Bay where MARGARET is berthed. Ronnie, Jimmy, and Magic make this trip five days a week regardless of the weather. The State does not allow seeding on Saturday or Sunday.

As Jimmy turns on the cabin lights and proceeds to fire up the ever-present kerosene heater, Ronnie tells me we will dredge seed oysters from Cedar Cove in the Little Choptank River and then transport them to Wildground Bar up and across the Bay on the Western Shore near Shady Side, Maryland. We will return to the slip in about 12 hours.

Jimmy begins to construct a three-sided corral around the deck by placing "gates" along the sides of the vessel from amidship forward about 35 feet. The open end will be toward the bow. On this day, approximately 650 bushels of seed oysters will be dredged from the bottom and dumped on MARGARET's deck for portage up the bay. Some of the large boats will load over 1,000 bushels per trip.

Ronnie Fithian is 37 years old and looks like actor Nick Nolte under a baseball cap. He is open and friendly. I am very comfortable aboard his boat and I do not feel like a stranger. He made his living catching rockfish year round for almost 20 years. With the state moratorium on catching the species, he has had to turn to clamming and the oyster seed program to make a living on the water.

"If you want to talk about rockfish, I'll go 'til I'm blue in the face," he said, "because when they done away with the rock, they done away with the fin fish market for the Bay, far as I'm concerned. No other fish could support the fishery the way the rockfish done."

"There's a few boys catching white perch and yellow perch, but you can't make any money. They only bring 10 to 15 cents a pound and people don't really eat them the way they ate rock. Men used to oyster, clam, or fish. Then, when oysters went bad they would fish. When the moratorium went into effect, there was no fish. So, we come off this bad winter for oysters and men are forced to stay in a bad industry because there wasn't nowhere else to go."

As we approach Cedar Cove, there are five large vessels dredging for shells, or seed oysters, within an area marked by bright orange flags. Jimmy is in his oilskins and preparing to put the dredge overboard. The "bucket" is attached to a line on the end of the long gaff pole similar to a spinnaker pole on a sailboat. Ronnie lowers and raises the dredge by using hydraulic controls in the cabin.

The five boats are working in tight formation. It is wet and dangerous work for the crewmen on deck. If the dredge boom swings and hits Jimmy, it will knock him overboard with ease. Suddenly, as I peer to the portside (left), I am shocked to see the vessel STERLING from Smith Island coming within two feet of our bow. Ronnie guns the engine in reverse and the STERLING turns quickly to starboard (right). Business continues as usual and I am still standing there with my mouth open, speechless. The boats in this fleet are "Smith Islanders" according to Ronnie as he breaks his silence for a brief moment. For the next several hours he must locate good shell beds, steer the boat, operate the dredge's hydraulic controls, and watch out for the other boats. Magic and I stay out of the way. I, for one, decide to become invisible for the time being.

As Ronnie repeats the procedure, he adds another distraction, the radio. He is talking to other captains working in the oyster-seeding fleet. Topics this early in the morning range from weather, to location of drops, to assurances that all boats are in good shape.

"Real watermen will continue to make a decent livin' even in hard times. Those that walk in because they think they're watermen will walk back out," Fithian says.

"There are many hardworking watermen making a real good living. There's watermen grossing $100,000 a year and there's watermen that can't pay the goddamn mortgage. Those that manage their time and plan to make it in the seafood industry will survive. Like farming, there's people losing farms everyday, but hell, there's other farmers buying them up. Hardworkers don't have to 'poor mouth' themselves. Some will be weeded out because it's going to get tougher and a damn sight more competitive. But I'll tell you the truth, I don't know of any occupation that I could replace my salary with in most small towns."

Fithian, like other watermen, has a personal problem with development and what it's doing to the quality of the Bay and his way of life. His home town of Rock Hall is a typical small, water-oriented community. Its residents, for the most part, make their living off the water.

"Developers come into town and start saying the industry is dying. They use that as a way to get sympathy for this ain't an industry worth savin'. They say, 'We'll help you by helping you get other work and creating jobs.' That's bullshit! If you take any business out of Rock Hall or Crisfield or Deal Island or any town like this, the town will keep rolling along. But, you take the seafood industry out to make room for condo developments and the like and there will be tumbleweeds rolling through that son-of-a-bitch in no time at all. And, besides, the seafood business ain't that bad at all!"

"I had a developer come to me as president of the Kent County Watermen's Association and say, 'We need your support for our project and in return we'll give the watermen forty boat slips for their boats.' Hell, you think I'm goin' to sell out this town for forty damn boat slips so he can turn the place upside down?"

"Rock Hall is more than a town to me. I've walked barefoot from one end of her to the other. I've got relatives and friends all over and 60% of our town is elderly. She's not a town, she's my life, my memories, and a big piece of my heart. And this developer wants to change that—he can go to hell.

"The word 'enough' is not in the developers vocabulary. If you gave them 90 percent of a town to develop, in six months they'd be back for the other ten percent," Fithian said.

On the day we are having this conversation aboard the MARGARET, the Somerset County Circuit Court temporarily blocked construction of a townhouse development on remote Smith Island, one of the few relatively tourist-free spots on Chesapeake Bay.

Judge Theodore R. Eschenburg Sr. said Somerset County's Board of Zoning Appeals had not given the public enough opportunity to comment on the development proposed. The Board approved the project to build 100 waterfront townhouses, a swimming pool and an 80-slip marina on 83 acres near the watermen's town of Ewell in September of 1987.

Eschenburg said in the ruling filed that the county handled the zoning application procedure so poorly that it should be started over. Opponents said a vacation community would alter the culture of the island, one of the few in the Chesapeake that is relatively free of tourism and development. Life in the three marshy towns that make up the island is dependent on crabs, fish, and oysters. The mainland is ten miles away, accessible only by water.

Yvonne Marshall Harrison, an islander, said she wasn't pleased that the developer "wanted to change things, and he don't live here."

She said one of those changes would come in the informal governance of the island. "The only government on the island is through our church," she said. "Outsiders would not abide by that."

Mrs. Harrison said her elderly mother was growing afraid of the "influx of strange people and what would come to pass" next door if the development were allowed. Fithian would agree.

"I'm not against well-planned slow development where people can get used to change. But I'm against these guys who say they have come to help us, to change our way of life for the better. Who the hell are they to change my way of life?" he said.

Fithian recognizes that changes are coming quickly. His own son is eight years old and he will introduce him to the water in a year or so. "I won't discourage or encourage him. We'll know soon enough whether he has a calling for the water in his blood. If he does fine, if he doesn't that's fine too. But he has to have an education so his options are open," he said.

When talk centers on seafood harvests, Fithian again expounds on his love for the fin fish industry. He disagrees with the state, Department of Natural Resources, and many conservation groups on their theories about the commodity on which he has depended for his livelihood.

"When you talk about seafood the first thing that comes out of DNR's mouth is 'overharvesting,'" he says. "Herring and the American shad are thick up and down the east coast—DNR put a moratorium on 'em nine or ten years ago because the numbers were decreasing. Same with yellow perch. These fish wouldn't have all come back to the Bay if it was overharvested. Hell, sunfish, pike, herring, shad, and rock used to be plentiful. Not now. But they didn't get overharvested. We didn't really want to catch those fish except rock. The real problem was and is pollution because there's no spawning," he said.

"We had meeting after meeting on the rockfish and how to handle a moratorium. Everybody agreed on a 55 percent catch limit. We went home one night and the next morning woke up to read in the paper that it was 100 percent. You think I trust government?"

"I saw a show on the TV on the salmon. There were 100 Indians upriver fishing and 10,000 hook and liners (recreational fishermen) at the mouth grabbing the fish when they came in. The Indians were blamed for overharvesting!! It's the same here with sport fishermen and watermen," Fithian said.

The dredging procedure continued as we talked. With Fithian, as others, I am in awe of his analogies, metaphors, and sheer logic. They often reduce issues to the simplest of terms and, more often then not, they make incredible sense. I am reminded of Dr. Rita Caldwell when she told the Sea Grant Advisory Board that we had better start listening to these men.

Fithian recognizes that, in the past, the image portrayed of the

Maryland watermen is often one of hard drinking, hard swearing, hard fighting, and hard working independent "cowboys on the water." "Years ago you could make $200 to $400 a day when oysters and fishin' was good. Some drank it up in their idle time. Nowadays if you're goin' to make it in this business, you better spend your time on the Bay and not in the bars," he says.

Wherever we went to dredge, the other boats ended up in the same congregation. "We must have a magnet on this boat," Jimmy yells to the cabin. The Captain laughs and yells back, "Hold on to her, I'm gettin' the hell out of this mess." Four boats are almost within an arm's reach.

Shortly after 8:00 a.m., Fithian tells Jimmy the MARGARET is about loaded. It's risky carrying heavy shell up the Bay in rough weather because of the potential for capsizing and he wants to play it safe. Jimmy locks the dredge in place and we move over to the spot where the State inspector will calculate the size of the load and give Ronnie a ticket, or receipt, for his work. The ticket reflects a load of 660 bushels at 97 cents a bushel. Ronnie will get a check in the mail in a few days for $640.20 for today's effort. That will be used to pay Jimmy his share, the boat it's share and the captain his share. The daily expenses on the MARGARET are not too bad . . . 50 gallons of fuel, sodas, and wear on equipment. It's the boat's mortgage, and major repairs that eat up a lion's share of the money he makes over five week's time. He doesn't carry insurance. It's a gamble without insurance, but Fithian feels he could be insurance poor if he tried to acquire it for a 76-year-old wooden vessel.

As we head out of the Little Choptank River, the sky darkens and the wind is picking up. Rain is not a problem on the Bay—wind is. It can easily turn the Bay from placid calm to aggressive four- and five-foot waves.

Jimmy comes into the cabin and takes off his oilskins. He turns his rubber gloves inside out and holds them over the kerosene heater to dry out. "Sit down with me and take a load off your mind," he says.

Jimmy is about 30 years old, stands just over five feet tall and weighs in the neighborhood of 140 pounds. He works as an oyster diver/crew in the winter, as crew with Fithian for the spring oyster seed program, and will run over 200 of his own crab pots from May through October.

He is from Rock Hall and loves his life on the water. He broke his back in a motorcycle accident ten years ago and still has problems lifting heavy weights.

"I can't shovel no oysters for three or four hours and I can't work on no skipjack. It's too hard. I don't have any problems on this boat because Ronnie helps me with the heavy stuff. He's a right nice captain," Jimmy exclaims as he leaves the gloves to prepare some ravioli which will be warmed, with the gloves, on the top of the kerosene heater. He will eat a sandwich and a piece of cake at mid-afternoon. In over 12 hours, Fithian will eat one apple and drink three or four diet sodas—he is preoccupied with other issues . . . least of all a 20- to 25-knot wind building up as we enter the main Bay.

A captain calls over the radio to see if we knew that the U.S. bombed Iranian ships. Ronnie says 'no' and Jimmy explains we should "drop the bomb if it's true. Reagan will do it. Damn Carter wanted to shoot peanuts." The next three hours would be filled with a variety of opinions on politics, racism, development, the economy, children, people in general and specific individuals, drug abuse, and more.

As we approach the Bay's Western Shore, two sailboats are off to our portside. All of a sudden Ronnie yells, "Is that a damn submarine? Damn it is and that Iran situation is worse than I thought!"

Another call comes over the radio and a Smith Islander asks, "Captain Ronnie, we ain't haulin' no seed oysters to Iran are we?"

"Reckon that submarine is leadin' the way? That'd be a $1 a bushel run if we was," the Captain responds in laughter. Jimmy is outside with his camera taking pictures of the rare grey object looming several hundred yards in front of us.

Waves are breaking across the deck and rain is coming down at a steady pace when we reach the oyster bar where the seed oysters are to go overboard. Like the dredge area, this spot on the Western Shore in Anne Arundel County has boundaries established by orange flags.

Jimmy has his oilskins back on and moves out into the rain to drag a fire hose three-inches in diameter across the pile of shells toward the front of the boat. He will use the hose's stream of water to blow the shells overboard, a process that will take about an hour.

Once the hose is forward, Fithian asks me to take the wheel so that he can go forward to help remove the gates that have held the shells on board. With this wind I am reluctant at the wheel, especially when I watch Ronnie sprinting across the pile and standing on the edge on a shifting mound of oyster shell. A quick vision is this man going overboard and me standing at the wheel of a 57-foot boat loaded with seed oysters in the middle of a Chesapeake squall. It's a bad thought for all concerned!

Moments later the Captain safely returns to the cabin and Jimmy is on his knees straddling the hose between his legs. As waves and spray pour over him he shoots a strong stream of water into the base of the pile. Shells fly overboard and will continue to do so until all have disappeared from the deck. Most boats in the seed oyster program must have crew shovel the shell overboard. It takes three men about two hours of steady shoveling with a load the size of the MARGARET's. The fire hose method is much more efficient.

By 1:00 p.m., the shells are gone and we head back to the Little Choptank River and Madison Bay. Jimmy sleeps most of the way and I talk to Ronnie or stare out into the Bay. It has also stopped raining as we approach the Eastern Shore. Commenting on a beautiful home spotted along the waterfront surrounded by luscious acreage, I am interrupted by Fithian. "You can believe that son-of-a-bitch don't haul seed oysters for a livin'." It will be 8:00 p.m. when I arrive at home.

Oh Chesapeake you
    mythical mistress
    protecting your children
who come calling
    and crying
helpless without your embrace
accept me
    as a stranger
among your midst
I promise
    I won't be here long.

MSB

Gill netting for rockfish. The watermen were hired by the state to do fish counts. The moratorium on harvesting the famed fish continues.

Crewman Eddie Ford empties an eel pot aboard Traveler.

Eel pots are stored by crewman Eddie Ford aboard Captain Bill Lampkin's Traveler.

Crewman Eddie Ford of *Traveler* rests after pulling eel pots off Baltimore's Hart-Miller Island.

Picking crabs at a Hooper's Island packing house.

Engine repairs and maintenance never end for the watermen.

Patent tong rigs sit in Annapolis harbor. Mayor Dennis Colahan allowed them free berths because of the poor harvest.

Prior to crabbing season, pots are made or repaired and stacked in backyards.

"Watermen can survive the natural cycles of things. Pollution, development and population are what's hurtin' our way of life. I ain't sayin' it's wrong. Some of us understand it better than others."

chapter 6

after oystering

Making a Living

It used to be, years ago when Bill Cummings, Ronnie Fithian, and others made a good living off the fishing industry, that many men never gave a thought to oystering, crabbing, or clamming. They made a living off catching more than the famed rock or striped bass . . . they caught shad, herring, eel, catfish, and perch. A comparison of major species landings figures gives an indication of where the Maryland fishery is and the impact it has on those who work it commercially to earn a living.

	1965 Harvest	1985 Harvest
American shad	1,343,000 lbs	CLOSED
River herring	2,092,000 lbs	104,000 lbs (1987)
Striped bass	2,949,000 lbs	CLOSED
Yellow perch (CLOSED 1987)	214,600 lbs	43,600 lbs
White perch	1,449,800 lbs	458,000 lbs
Eels	195,000 lbs	74,000 lbs

Trapping Eels

Consider Bill Lampkins, 36, a Grasonville waterman who started trapping eels in 1982. While there is no American market for the slippery creatures, eels up to two feet long are considered quite a delicacy in Europe where they will bring an average of $10 a pound. Lampkins and other eelers can expect their price to fluctuate between 65 cents and $2.65 per pound depending on the supply.

I wanted to go eeling so on April 27 at 6:00 a.m. I met Bill Lampkins at the County Dock beside the Kent Narrows Bridge. He arrived with his mate, 19-year-old Eddie Ford. Lampkins greeted me warmly and immediately expressed his disappointment with the present eel catches because the market is excellent and the prices are high. He is simply having a hard time finding eels. He has several hundred cylindrical-shaped eel pots up on the Chester River and about 150 over in the Baltimore Inner Harbor. He and Ford placed the pots in the Inner Harbor, for the first time, about 36 hours ago. The Harbor area is dotted with many dilapidated pilings and piers that make it dangerous for the men but potentially good for eels. The water quality is poor. It's a gamble to try and find eels there but it's worth the risk.

"They may have a pattern, but they're so unpredictable—you can't guess 'em out. It only takes one night for 'em to break out of the mud and if you hit that night you're in luck. If not, you collect your pots and move somewhere else," Lampkins says. Eels remain submerged beneath the bottom mud until the weather warms up and instinct has them move out into the water system.

"You have to make it anyway you can," Lampkins says as he prepares to eel seven days a week from May until November. "There's no such thing as makin' up for a bad winter. If you made money everyday, everybody'd be a waterman. Even at its best, it's hard work."

Lampkins' boat, TRAVELER, is in the slip closest to the Kent Narrows drawbridge on Maryland's Eastern Shore. He likes this slip out of the hundred or so that the Queen Anne's County government provides for commercial watermen because it has plenty of room on either side of his 40-foot boat for two eel live boxes which are 3 feet by 6 feet by 3 feet plywood containers that hold the eels until they are bought by a processor. A drawback to the slip is the strong current coming through the narrows which makes it difficult to berth the boat—easily moving her away from a straight course he steers between pilings. A small frustration, admittedly, but one he must contend with every day he returns home.

There is no real season for eeling in the Chesapeake Bay area. The few dozen men who catch eel will play it pretty much the way Lampkins does: "We'll lay traps on 6,000 feet of line (rope). Some in the Chester River, some in the Inner Harbor and see what we do. Eels are crazy. You don't find 'em, believe you just bump into each other. If we collide with 'em we'll have a good strike," he said. "They can be here today and gone tomorrow."

Eels are bringing a little over $2.50 a pound and the buyers are so anxious to get them they will send trucks down to the docks up to three times a week "even if it's to collect only a hundred pounds," Lampkins says.

Bill and his mate Eddie Ford have been at the marina since about 5:30 a.m. They came early to talk to other men about eels and see what the rumors were on the water. The eels should start moving with warm water but the weather this April has been fluctuating to a point where Bill says both he and the eels are frustrated.

We proceed to load five bushel baskets of soft clams on TRAVELER which will be used to bait the eel trap pots and two large 55 gallon trash cans. The cans will be used to store each of the two 6,000 foot trot lines which will have a pot attached about every 20 yards and placed on the bottom of the river.

Bill Lampkins is a warm and friendly man whose enthusiasm for working on the water is anything but subtle. He speaks quickly and has an optimistic, excited uplift to his sentences. He has been eeling for seven years, although he has only owned TRAVELER since August 1987. He is very open about his pride in this workboat.

"I saved my money doing everything I could on the water to buy her last August. She cost out about $80,000 with the Robbins hull, Detroit diesels, and all the electronics. I rent my house and own my boat. Is that a weird sense of prosperity!"

Eddie Ford has been working on the Bay since he was six and going out with his waterman father. Bill got into the business by chance. "I was working construction down Virginia Beach and one rainy day, when we weren't workin', I walked into this dive shop. The man told me I could make $200 a day diving for oysters in the Chesapeake. I said he was full of crap and only wanted to sell me the equipment. Hell, I bought it though, came to Kent Island and have been oyster divin' each winter ever since." In the winter, Bill dives for oysters on Eddie's grandfather's boat. Eddie dives for someone else!

As we leave the slip, we head through the Narrows and into the Chester River, Bill says that the seafood industry is on the decline and has been for some time. Like other men working on the water he continues to hope it will "come back," but in the meantime, will put in extra days and longer hours.

"Yesterday we pulled and moved pots from 5:30 a.m. 'til 8:30 p.m. Sunup to sundown and when I go lay down in bed after all them hours at the wheel, I still hear the engine and feel the vibration," he said.

Of laying pots in Baltimore's Inner Harbor he said, "it will be the last time. It's a filthy place. Burn your eyes from industry plants and they even had a boat goin' round pickin' up trash around those expensive yachts in the marina. We haven't caught narry an eel up there so those pots are comin' out. I believe I like the country a whole lot better than that neck of the woods. I'd like to have it the way it was around here 50 years ago when there was a lot of workin' watermen and no condos or traffic. But I guess that's prosperity—or so they say."

Bill and Eddie have been eeling for about a month and the best day they have had this season was 400 pounds. The eels were caught in pots that had set beneath the surface for three days when the air temperature was in the 70 to 75 degree range the first week of April. That works out to $1,000 over three days or about $350 a day. It cost him over $200 a day in expenses to work. He figures until the eels break from the mud he will average about 200 pounds a day which "is not discouraging this early in the season, but this time last year we were doin' 1,500 pounds a day the first couple of weeks, then it slacked off."

I spot orange flags in the Chester River that mark one of the oyster seed beds the men from the Oyster Replenishment Program will plant this week. Bill points out that the oyster seed will be planted right beside a clam line boundary and that if the clammer crosses over they will scrape or dredge the new seed. A small point, but to him it would make more sense to separate the two.

"Clammin' is just like goin' to the bank," he says of his colleagues. "Every day a steady $400 to $600 and in by lunch time. Don't make a fortune, but it's goin' to the bank a few days a week. I don't want to do no clammin', but it's really the only game in town that's steady right now."

"If you only work on the water for the money you won't make it. Too many dry spells. Ups and downs. You do it 'cause you love it out here. I'll do this as long as I can feed my family and shelter them. I ain't goin' to become no street person like on T.V. I hope I can keep doin' it forever," he says.

He illustrates the changing face of the waterfront communities by giving me an example: "I live in an older community of mostly workin' men, but my landlord won't let me keep my eel pots in the yard anymore—says it will run down the neighborhood. I believe that's a hell of a sign of change when a waterman can't keep his gear in his yard."

Bill spots one of his buoy markers which means the beginning of his first trotline. I am eager to see the winder reel in the pots that contain eel for market. Bill will set a total of 1,100 eel pots on almost seven miles of trotline this season. Today we will work with about 200 pots he has in the Chester River.

As Eddie begins the ritual of rubber boots, gloves, and oilskin coveralls, Bill moves to the aft control station. Eddie will pull the pots from the line as the winder engine brings them to the surface and up over the side of the boat. He will empty the eels into a large plastic rectangular basket with two-inch diameter holes on the bottom. They then drop into a large holding box in the center of TRAVELER's deck. The holding box can hold a ton of eels. On about the eighth pot, Eddie has a full pot with two eels spilling into the plastic basket. Bill expresses his joy by shouting, "Whoo-whee! Everytime you see one of those big boys it's like lookin' $2.50 right between the eyes!"

The rest of the 80 pots on this line would not yield as much enthusiasm as many are empty or contain but a few small eels in the eight-inch range. The total poundage from this trotline, after a four-day set in the river is only about 150 pounds and Eddie comments that "one good pot don't make up for all them empty ones we pulled." Bill is more optimistic, responding that "the Chester River has been real kind the last few years—good eelin' and it will get better when the water gets over 50 degrees."

Bill makes all his own pots during the winter or when he can't work. He can make about 20 pots a day, and they cost him about $7 each. I quickly figure that he has about $8,000 and at least two month's of his personal time only in pot fabrication. He has to make the pots because he can't afford to buy them at $15 to $20 each. During the course of the season he will lose about one-third of them to weather and recreational boat traffic.

As we move TRAVELER up the river to where the next trotline is set, Eddie takes a break in the cabin. He relaxes at the dinette and puts a pinch of Skoal Long-Cut chewing tobacco between his cheek and gum. Neither man smokes and the cabin is neat and clean. Eddie uses a plastic champagne cup to spit in. When we reach the trotline, the tobacco will be replaced by a piece of bubble gum.

The next line proves more disappointing than the first. I find myself eagerly awaiting each pot as it breaks the surface and I hope of a good strike. I also begin to share the disappointment when pot after pot reveals little, and the rush of elation when one is full.

Bill speculates that today's catch will be enough for spending money to go to southern Maryland to talk to the eelers and check out marinas to berth TRAVELER should he decide to move everything to warmer water in the south for a couple of weeks.

"We'll drive down to St. Mary's County tonight and talk to some men. I need to do it personally because you can't believe anything you hear on the water. If they're doin' good we can move all our gear down by boat, truck, and trailer and set up our operation in a day," he said.

"Last year I worked up the Potomac and down on the James River in Virginia. The men down there said 'those eels will laugh at you puttin' them round traps in.' On the Potomac the men use the square pots, a little like crab pots, but I had 1,100 round and ran em' for ten days before I caught a thing. First I thought those boys was right, but I proved 'em a little wrong. I'll tell you how crazy eels are, you put all square pots on cork floats out there and put one round pot in with 'em. The square ones could fill up and not either an eel in the round one. I swear you can't figure 'em out. It's all a gamble, but I do believe them eels do laugh at us most of the time!"

The move to the Potomac and Patuxent Rivers would be a gamble too. "I could leave here Friday, thinkin' the grass is greener down there and Saturday the Chester River could be full of eels," he said. I think back to oyster dredging on the ELSWORTH when Captain Gene Tyler took the MARTHA LEWIS down to Solomons to see if the catch might be better. These men are constantly thinking of new approaches to try and outsmart the weather, the harvest, or the Bay—always hoping that one change will increase their luck and give them the edge over small or large, real or imagined adversaries.

As TRAVELER's winder engine pulled in the line and the silver clothespin-like hooks surfaced dangling a pot tied to a cloth funnel, Ford would grab the pot, dunk it once in the river to rinse off the silt, open the clip and funnel dump the eels in the holding box and then rebait. Rebaiting the trap with a handful of soft-shelled razor clams would be followed by retying and setting the pin before passing it back to Lampkins who would prepare them for a new set. Today, however, the men will not rebait because of the scouting trip to southern Maryland. Lampkins is stacking the 200 pots neatly in the stern of the boat.

In the spring, bait can stay in the pots for a week but in the summer with warmer water, it goes bad and must be replaced daily—which cost a great deal of money in time, gas, and clams.

Lampkins uses three primary buyers for his eels; one from Delmarva, one from the Rock Hall and his principal buyer, George Robberecht of Montrose, Virginia. Once Robberecht's trucks leave with Lampkins' eel, they will go to the factory. Once there they will be purged in clean water and put on ice where they will remain dormant during a direct airplane flight to Europe.

After retrieving all the pots, we head back to the Narrows, keeping an eye on a storm building in the west; Bill tells Eddie to prepare for the trip to St. Mary's. He invites me back again and re-emphasizes that they will be working seven days a week until August when it's so hot the eels "drop off."

Eddie says he's "takin' a vacation and not doin' a lick a work during two weeks in August." "I haven't taken a vacation in seven years," Bill says. "I like it too much out here on the water. Maybe a trip to the Caribbean in the winter when I'm lookin' at the ice and snow out here. But I always got work to do so who knows."

At the dock I help Eddie open the livebox alongside the pier and hold it steady while he takes netfull after netfull of the gray-green eels from a livebox on the deck and empties them into the livebox. A couple of hundred pounds later he is finished and after hosing down the boat, prepares to leave with Bill.

"You can go eeling with us anytime, but if you go 10,000 more times it will be the same process as today. Hopefully though, next time we'll fill that box for ya!"

They will unload the traps in the yard of a fellow waterman, head for St. Mary's County, and probably return to the Island very late this evening. I am going to Tilghman to talk to some crab potters. I wonder if Bill Lampkins will move his entire operation to the Potomac and Patuxent Rivers to "collide" with eels.

The Not-so-Lazy Days of May

Several developments began to take shape for the watermen in May.

First, watermen are reporting frequent sightings of rockfish and the Maryland Striped Bass White Paper Committee is mapping out indications of what fishing will be like for the famed fish once the present moratorium is lifted. The committee is responsible for figuring out a plan that will be equitable to the commercial fishermen, sportsfishermen, and charterboat captains while safeguarding the species itself.

Maryland's rockfish moratorium plan stipulates that the fishery must be opened to both sports and commercial fishermen. This is not a popular mandate. Surveys have shown that 85 percent of the rock were caught in nets, 15 percent by sports fishermen and four percent by charterboats. The charterboat captains want a more equitable share of the rockfish "pie." While all seem to agree that the rock population will not reach that of the days of yore, the commercial watermen are very clear in expressing their interests because it is how they make their living. They want:

- A license freeze that would delay entry into the commercial fishery. Before being licensed, newcomers would have to prove they fished for a living two years under someone else's license.
- A gill net season; suggested is November 1 to March 15.
- Closing of commercial fishing on weekends; no nets could be set

or pulled from sunrise Saturday through sunset Sunday to discourage entry by part-timers who hold regular jobs and fish commercially only on weekends.

- Gear reduction to limit maximum individual net quotas to 3,333 yards.
- Closure of all fishing, sports and commercial, during the spawning run.

The Department of Natural Resources promises that all interested parties will have their say before all this is over. Dr. Paul Massicot, who heads fisheries, said committee decisions are subject to review by the Atlantic States Marine Fisheries Commission, which will also have much to say about harvests. Much later will come public hearings and meetings. Larry Simns says the watermen will be ready.

Second, soft-shell clams continued to make their remarkable two-year comeback in the Bay. Watermen this spring are catching their 15-bushel limit by breakfast time. The downside of the clam market, however, is that the plentiful clams have caused a glut in the market, thus, the packers starting the price war previously mentioned and the clammers holding out for more money—at least more than the $20 per bushels they have been getting. "A lot of our people (Marylander's) don't know that you eat the damn things," said Jerry Harris of W. H. Harris Seafood, Inc. By contrast, Harris went to a show in California recently and said they could not fry enough for the people wanting them. Not so on the Chesapeake, however, where Maryland waters produced about half of the nation's 7.5 million pounds of soft-shell clam meat in 1987. For example, United Shellfish on the Chesapeake's eastern shore sent 2,500 gallons of shucked clams to New England the week of May 9th, while only 24 gallons were shipped to United's Maryland customers. I found these statistics difficult to believe—but true!

Nevertheless, clams are plentiful for the time being, and if the Maryland Department of Agriculture's Office of Seafood Marketing moves to promote clams in Maryland, nationally and to the Far East, the watermen may see another temporary windfall. But, who knows, as the watermen say you can't out-guess Mother Nature and she could reverse things in a hurry at any time.

Third, in May the Department of Natural Resources will definitely propose a set of yellow perch fishing restrictions by July.

DNR officials say the perch population is declining to dangerous lows and the catch has got to be decreased. Since the striped bass moratorium went into effect, the yellow perch has become an important catch to Maryland's few remaining commercial fishermen, who say that DNR's proposed reduction of the catch is based on insufficient data and that no valid research effort has been directed at the fish.

An initial DNR proposal was met by determined resistance, and DNR withdrew all proposals with the intention of rewriting them. The DNR held public hearings on proposed new regulations, the last of which was held on April 12.

The best guess anyone can make is that environmental factors have caused the yellow perch population to decline through reproduction failure, although biologists say they don't know why.

Sportfishermen and watermen alike want to see this decline end, but sportfishing interests want to see commercial fishing stop immediately, so the fish would be preserved for them until the state figures out what's gone wrong. I suppose everyone wants first to protect their own turf, and the selfishness characteristic of man in general will make processes like this more difficult.

"Chances are a moratorium won't bring back the yellow perch until we find out what's wrong," said C. Don Auld, a member of the Sportfisheries Advisory Committee.

Watermen also want guarantees that if the state restricts the catch, they'll solve the problem of the decline. "If they can show us they do something about the real problem, we could live with the restrictions," said Larry Simns, president of the Maryland Watermen's Association. "But you can't continue to say 'Give up the species,'" he said.

Although pollution and acid rain are believed to be major contributors to the decline, biologists admit they know little about the fish and its habits.

If DNR could better coordinate its research, "we wouldn't sit in hearings deciding whose gonna catch the last fish," Simns said.

On May 22, I went to Sandy Point State Park to work all day at the Annual Chesapeake Bay Fest, a fundraising and "awareness of the Bay" day. The politicians were out in force as approximately 65,000 people attend the all-day festivities which begin at 7:30 a.m. with a runner's race across the Bay Bridge. The Maryland Watermen's Association has the seafood and drink concessions; I would work the beer truck with my staff assistant and consistent volunteer, Pati DuVall and Bob Slaff, president of the Marine Trades Association of Maryland. There was little time for talk of issues—the order of the day was raising money for the MWA so they could maintain active legislative, public relations, and education programs. Efforts this day would raise about $15,000 for the MWA coffers.

The first step in promoting clams to the Maryland residents, part of the Department of Agriculture's Seafood Marketing Office, was in effect at Bay Fest—a young woman from the MWA walked through throngs of fest-goers asking if they would like to try a fried clam. There were a few takers, but I was still under the impression that Marylanders "need to be sold" further—the clams didn't quite look enough like French fries!

I can sit
    seemingly passive
gazing at far horizon.

Slowly, settling whitecaps
beckon me
    to ancient harvests,
my thoughts turn
    to times gone by.
There will be another dawn
like yesterdays
caught in the loneliness
    of open water
        silently searching
her depths and desires
to reach her life blood
    which will also be mine. . .

MSB

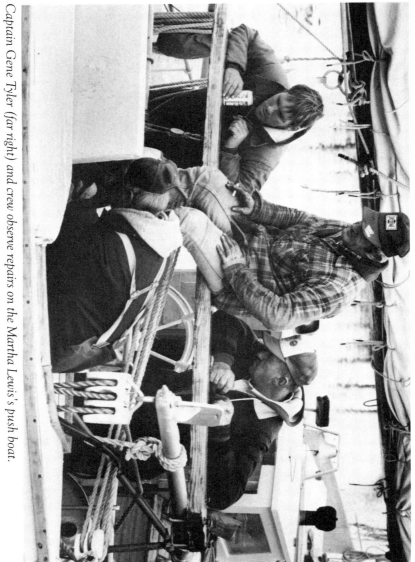

Captain Gene Tyler (far right) and crew observe repairs on the Martha Lewis's push boat.

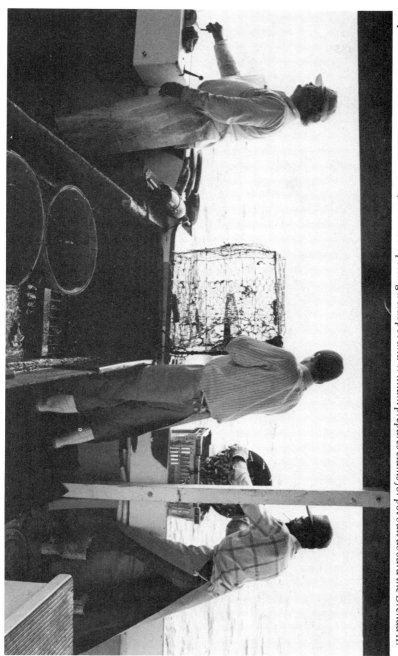

Captain Robbie Wilson is at the helm, Brian is inspecting a crabpot and William prepares clams for pot bait aboard the Brenda II.

As Captain Robbie Wilson steers the Brenda II in position to pull a new pot, William empties a crabpot and Brian sorts crabs.

Captain Robbie Wilson searches the way for his next line of crabpots as William baits a pot before sending it overboard at Robbie's direction.

William (left) and Brian stacking crab pots on the wooden roof canopy of the Brenda II. The pots will be stored until they are relocated in a new location on the Bay.

Chesapeake Blue Crabs are the spice of life for many, but the watermen are the ones with a little salt water in their veins. Unloading crabs at a Hooper's Island packing house.

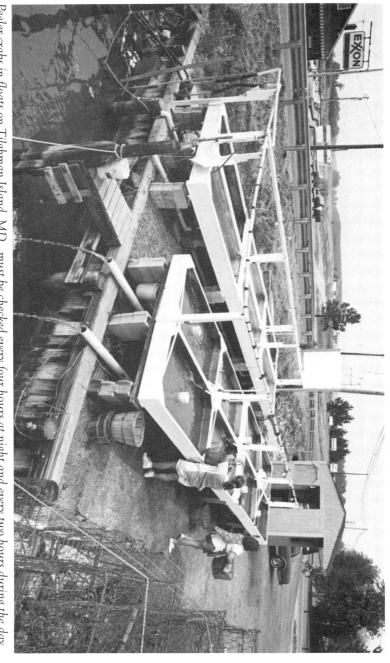

Peeler crabs in floats on Tilghman Island, MD., must be checked every four hours at night and every two hours during the day. The women work 24 hours a day seven days a week for the crabbing season.

Brenda Wilson illuminates her crabs peeler floats to see if any of the peeler crabs have turned to soft shells. It is 4:00 a.m. in the morning.

Hundreds of crabpots being loaded on boats preparing for a day on the Bay. Many men own from 600-1000 pots.

"Be hard to choose between which is more important, my boat, my truck or my woman . . . depends on the time of day."

chapter 7

crabbing into summer

The Life of the Blue Crab

When working on the water, ironies remain ever present. For the oystermen a rainy spring would help dissipate the spread of MSX and Dermo diseases by reducing the salinity of the Bay. The Bay area has been battered by unusually boisterous weather with quite a lot of rain in early May. But as of this writing, conditions have been poor. June's rainfall was virtually non-existent. July just as bad and forecasts seem dismal.

Men planning to harvest Maryland's famous blue crab either by crab pot or from trotline have, by and large, lost considerable time starting their harvest. Aside from the rainy, windy weather holding the men up on their operations, the weather affects the movement of crabs up the Bay from warmer southern waters. Colder than normal temperatures delayed migration which is generally in full swing by mid-May.

The high value of crabs and the frightening decline in rockfish, oysters, ducks, geese, shad, herring, and perch have caused concern. Crabbers and state agencies blame any number of possibilities: over-harvest, the effects of environmental conditions on crab stocks, waste in the fishery, and other conservation issues. Nevertheless, the blue crab is now the most valuable species caught in the Chesapeake.

Most crabs follow a specific rate of growth and time and distance of migration. However, as the watermen know from the slow start of this year's season, the effects from changing rainfall, temperature, and wind can cause crabs to spawn earlier or later than usual, migrate far-ther or closer up the Bay and her tributaries, migrate earlier or later, spawn in concentrated or wide-spread areas, or, in other areas, and generally deviate from normal patterns.

Nevertheless, the life history of the famous Chesapeake blue crab is fairly consistent. It begins with the hatching of larval crabs from the sponge of fertilized eggs carried by an adult female. Females will produce 2 million to 3 million more larvae, which are released in the water system in June, July, and August. These larvae begin to resem-ble a larger crab after about a month and seven to eight moltings or shedding of their hard shell. All crabs go into semi-hibernation dur-ing the winter, November to March. By the second summer, the crabs are reaching maturity, with the peak about 14 months from the original larvae stage. Of the millions of larvae produced, very few will survive to reproduce.

One of the interesting characteristics of the crab is the way nature has allowed us to determine its sex. Blue claws mean the crab is male. Red tips on the claws mean it's female. And there are many that point to the patriotic nature of the crab: mature females display a dome-shaped replica of the U.S. Capitol on their undersides, while males display an outline of the Washington Monument. Size of the crab is not an indication of gender.

One Dorchester County crabber working in Virginia waters this year is Harold Robinson, who ties up in Wingate, Maryland, and makes a 25-mile run south to work every morning. Robinson, 40, says this spring's weather is the worst he can remember, which may ac-count for his observation that "there's not a whole lot of crabs below the Virginia line, and they're very scarce on the Maryland side. Since the first of May, our average catch has been 25 bushels a day,"

Robinson said. The price he received May 5 was $55 for number ones—large male crabs—and $25 for females.

Robinson began crabbing on the seaside this year where he said he found plenty of crabs. "The he-crabs were fine, but the she-crabs were on the small side." The price was $22 for number one males and $10 for the rest, but the market was flukey. Robinson said he saw one buyer dump a truckload of crabs overboard because there was no market for them that day.

Bill Rice, who crabs in the Potomac River, said in the first week of May that his season started very slowly. He was getting only a bushel out of every 200 pots every day, he said May 3. "We're really not catching any crabs at all yet," he said, "when normally we are catching them now." A bushel of five-inch crabs was going for $50 in the first week of May on the Potomac River.

Many watermen will harvest hard crabs by using two-foot square pots made of chicken wire and framed with steel poles. Holes about four inches in diameter are placed in the sides of a pot, and there is a wire funnel on the interior for bait. Each pot is tied to a line from 12 to 60 feet in length with a cork float at the other end. Each float has the watermen's identification mark on it. The crabs, seeking food, enter through a hole and are trapped. The men will pull, empty, and rebait the pots each day and most will use from 600 to 1,000 pots. At a cost of about $15 per pot the venture is expensive, especially when they know they may lose 25 percent of their pots each season to bad weather and recreational boat propellers. Over 250,000 crab pots will be in use in Maryland during the 1988 season which will run until late October, at least. They will harvest 43,867,894 pounds of hard, soft and peeler crabs at a value of $25,242,074.93. Their hopes run high that 1989 will be even better.

Enough to Go Around?

On May 1, while some men from the southern Bay have dredged for crabs in Virginia waters similar to the method of dredging used by oystermen in the winter, Milton Parks, a veteran Tangier Island crabber pointed out that, the catch this spring is "as low as any time I can remember for this time of year. Production is so low it won't pay expenses." Because the crabbing effort has increased so much in recent years, Parks worries that there will not be enough crabs to go around. "I don't think that there are any more crabs down there (at the mouth of the Bay) than there were last year and there's more and more pots in the water," he said.

Parks quit crab dredging March 10 after a "fair" season and started potting in the last week of March. "From the first of April to the middle of the month, it was pretty good, then it died right off. It diminished to nothing in the first week of May." The first crab run usually lasts until late May, so crabbers are wondering "is that all there is?" to this economically vital part of their season. "A lot of the younger skippers are hurting," Parks said.

On Friday, May 6, the Tangier Island, Virginia crabbing fleet was taking between 9 and 14 bushels of crabs a boat. Only the price, $60 for number ones (large males) and $30 for sooks, or females, was making it possible for the boats to go out, Parks reported.

This spring, as Parks sees it, crabbers are caught between low production and high expenses after a crab-dredging season that was less profitable than in the past. "I quit earlier than I ever did because it was costing a minimum of $200 a day to operate and the bulk crabs aren't present like they used to be."

The cost of setting up for long-range crab potting may have deterred more Marylanders from working in Virginia waters. Parks said he's seen no more Maryland boats than have worked in his area before. Most are from Dorchester County, but he's seen some from as far north as Kent Island.

Chan Rippons, Sr. of Dorchester County is a crabbing expert. He has been crabbing all his life, and Rippons Brothers Seafood, which deals only in crabs, celebrates its 40th anniversary in 1988. In a conversation shared with Gail Dean of the Dorchester News, Rippons said that quite a bit has changed in 40 years.

"When I first went into the business," he said, "everything I bought was 'picked.' Then people began coming by from the city, picking out the best crabs before steaming to take home in bushel baskets and cook for themselves."

This led to the practice of sorting out the best crabs and backing them in slatted barrels for shipment to the city. Rippons said bay plants or vegetation were also packed in the barrels to keep the crabs alive during the trip. These first trips were made by steamboat, he said, but eventually trucks took over.

"You had to deliver them yourself to the wholesale fish market in Baltimore," Rippons said. "You couldn't put live crabs on a freight truck, because there were no guarantee what shape they would be in when they arrived at the market."

Rippons recalled catering huge crab feasts in Annapolis, where politicians feasted on dozens of bushels of the steaming delicacies. Some novices have trouble learning how to get inside the shell but not this crew, Rippons said, "They knew how to pick them and eat them."

"Watermen are the ones who developed the system of sorting crabs. This led to the pricing system where the largest males, number ones, get top dollar. Smaller males are classified as number twos while females, which are less desired for crab feasts, all fall into the sook category," he said.

In the days before the Fourth of July, crabs usually bring their top price of the season. Rippons said watermen get over $55 a bushel for number one crabs and $25 a bushel for sooks. This is another sign of change in the system. "I bought many a one for $1 a barrel," he said, with two and a half bushels of crabs to most barrels. Crabs are still sorted and sold in the same manner—males, females, large, medium, small.

A Day Crab Potting

On June 16, I left Annapolis at 2:10 a.m. to meet Captain Robbie Wilson aboard the BRENDA II for a day of crab potting. I was enthusiastic because I hoped I would see William, a crewman from the skipjack ELSWORTH, who would be working with Robbie.

I pulled into the marina on the north side of the Knapps Narrows drawbridge and Tilghman Island to find James dozing off in his truck. He arrived a few minutes before at 4:00 a.m. from Baltimore. At 4:15, Brenda Wilson's blue Caprice pulled into the parking lot. C.R., Robbie and Brenda's son, was going trotlining for crabs on his boat and Brenda was here to check on her "peeler" crabs. Robbie was behind them in his truck. He had already purchased ten bushels of soft clams at $12 a bushel which we would use for baiting the pots. William arrived about five minutes later and Brian, another crewman who lives on the BRENDA II, began to stir in the cabin.

At 4:30 a.m. we are on board and Robbie is moving his boat through the Narrows toward the Chesapeake. We will "fish" about 800 crab pots today. They have been sitting for three days because the crabs have been very slow coming up the Bay. And while Robbie has almost as many over on the western shore of the Bay, he doesn't want to leave these in any longer than two or three days.

"This is the scarcest I've ever seen it. The worst in my life. The best day of the season so far was the first day and it was only 14 bushels. We fish these pots 'til about 4:00 this evening and we'll be lucky if we break even," Robbie said.

At 4:40 a.m. Robbie, William, and Brian don their rubber aprons and long sleeved shirts to protect them from sea nettle stings, and rubber gloves. Robbie turns on a spotlight aimed 75 feet off the starboard bow and turns on the deck lights so we can see the work in progress. Except for these lights, the area is totally dark. He is steering and controlling the speed of his 45-foot crabbing boat from controls amidship on the starboard side. There is another control station at the rear of the vessel.

As we pull alongside the first floating buoy, Robbie snags it with a boat hook. He places the float on the side rail (washboard) and runs the line attached to the submerged pot into a 12-inch disc winder that, when he steps on a pedal on the deck, reels the line and pot toward the boat. Once the pot is free of the surface, he lifts it over a five-foot stainless steel roller that is attached to the side of the boat in front of the winder disc, grabs the pot, and hands it to William. William empties the crabs, sea nettles, toadfish, and anything else that swam into the pot into a three and a half by six foot wooden box containing two bushel baskets. Once he empties the pot, he shovels a couple of handfuls of clams into the pot's cylindrical bait chamber. By the time William does his job Robbie is alongside the next float. As he brings it into the boat, William throws the freshly baited pot into the Bay where the second pot came out. This way the floats stay in the same area each day and in a relatively straight line. Simultaneously, Brian at the culling box sorts the crabs William dumps. He inspects the flipper of each crab, a flipper which is white with a pink or red line running down it means the crab will shed its hard shell in a matter of days. These "peeler" crabs are placed in baskets behind Brian on the engine box cover. "Peelers" with the red or pink line go into one basket, ones with green go in another. All the peelers will go home to Miss Brenda via the soft crab/peeler floats which will hold them until they shed. While there is no limit to the number of crabs that can be harvested, there are requirements: minimum size is five inches across point-to-point for hard males, three-and-a-half inches for females, and three inches for peelers.

The process of pull, empty, rebait, and sort will go on every 15 to 20 seconds for the next 12 hours. James is asleep in the cabin waiting for daylight to break the horizon—wherever that is—and I think for a minute about William calling Robbie "Captain Midnight" when we worked on the skipjacks last winter.

Even though the pots have "set" for three days, one after another turns up empty. The crew is quiet. Robbie turns on the radio to listen and check with other captains. Several are complaining about the poor crabbing on the Western Shore. At 5:36 a.m., an hour after we started, the men have pulled over 100 pots. The harvest yields one-half bushel of large males, seven peelers, and only two females. Dismal . . .

If the oyster season ended with hope for a promising crab harvest, the last five weeks have not given the men much encouragement. "Last year I had days when we caught 99 bushels. Three pots would damn near fill a basket, and we went seven days a week knowing oysterin' was goin' to be bad, you know. But see, with all those large male crabs last year, we would pull in 30 bushels of 'em and only have one bushel of small ones. Without the small ones last year, you can't have many big ones this spring, you know," Robbie said.

"We're gettin' $55 a bushel for large males and $25 for females. I figure it cost me $300 a day to start my boat ($50 gas, $120 bait, crew, etc.). So averaging four or five bushels a day doesn't do any good. I'll tell ya if we average one or two good crabs in each pot we can make it with 800 pots, but I ain't doin' it nowadays. It's slow for sure but late July and August should pick up. I need a dollar's worth of crabs at least in each pot, but I ain't makin' 30 cents now," he said. "At $20 a pot in paint, zinc, and wire and goin' up all the time, I'd put 'em on shore for a while but there's no place to store 'em. Just as well leave 'em overboard and see how we make out," he says.

As the pots are pulled, I notice small crabs, maybe 2 to 3 inches long from point to point slipping through the chicken wire back into the Bay. Robbie explains that these small crabs are a good sign. "They'll shed about three or four times in the next month or so and then be about legal size of five inches," she says. There is hope for late summer after all he exclaims.

The last pot pulled had a broken clip holding the plastic flap covering the bait cylinder. Robbie spots the problem immediately, stops the operation, gets the tools and fixes the broken clip so William can rebait. He will make on-the-spot minor repairs on at least 50 pots today and the average repair time for this expert is about seven seconds.

We hear 13-year-old C.R. Wilson talking on the radio to various captains. He is upset that he's not catching the amount of crabs he wants. No one else is either. He doesn't know whether to put his trotline in a different location or leave it and wait for a change in tide which may bring in more crabs. I notice that the captains offer the boy encouragement and information to help him learn his trade. Robbie listens intently. He has not interfered.

A half-hour later C.R. is on the radio again and is still very frustrated. Robbie tells Brian to take the boat hook and pull the pots for William. He moves into the cabin to operate the boat's controls and the radio. Robbie calls his son.

"It's pitiful," C.R. exclaims in a child-like voice.

"Well, why don't you take yer line up and take her in then," Robbie says half sarcastically. "I have problems of my own out here," he says as C.R. immediately gets off the radio.

"He gets upset. He's learning but I let him know if he wants to be the captain of his own boat he has to roll with what happens. He caught more crabs than I did yesterday so he was braggin'. Today he's mad, you know. His crew didn't show up yesterday so he said he was going to 'beat him up.' I told him he can't do that. He's learnin,'" Robbie says.

He then calls his father "Big Daddy" who trotlines near C.R. and keeps an eye on him. "I think he's mad with me," Robbie says.

"I guess," Big Daddy explains. "He looks like he's goin' in."

As Robbie is talking, Brian holds the foot pedal for the power winder down too long and a crab pot flies up over the roller bar and hits him on the bridge of his nose. Robbie slams down the radio and William moves around the culling box. Brian's nose is bleeding but it's not broken. Within three minutes work continues. During this reprieve William turns on the FM radio for a rock 'n roll station in Washington D.C. "This jukebox distracts us from thinkin' about pullin' empty pots," he says.

"Hey, Mick," Robbie yells. "C'mere. I want you to see the Bay's only crabologist." As I peer off to starboard, I see the crabbing boat MISS LISA coming towards us. Captain Leroy and his mate are on board.

"Hey, Leroy," Robbie yells. "I want Mick to meet you. Told him you were the Bay's only crabologist!" Leroy laughs. He is in his late 20's and lives on Tilghman. "When he went to his high school reunion, members of his class said they were either one kind of professional or another," Robbie says, "So ol' Leroy said he was a crabologist instead of a damn ol' crabber." They both laugh and Leroy pulls away. "We'll never let him live that down," Robbie says.

At 8:13 a.m. Robbie cuts the engine back and takes off his gloves and apron. He asks William if he's hungry. The men go in for sandwiches and sodas, leaving only two bushels of crabs behind them on the deck. As Robbie eats his ham sandwich, he talks on the radio to other captains. At 8:19 a.m. Robbie gets up and puts his apron back on. I'm still eating and so are the others. After six minutes the break is over. Uneaten sandwiches are wrapped in foil to be finished later.

The pulling continues until Robbie suddenly cuts the engine again. He ran over one of his pot lines and his propeller cut it quickly. William reaches below and pulls a 100-foot "drag line" out of a bushel basket. The line has hooks that look like umbrellas every four feet and a weight near the end. Robbie throws it in the water and begins dragging the Bay bottom in smaller and smaller circles hoping to snag the lost crab pot. It cost $15, so it's worth the time to look for it. After 15 minutes he gives up. The pot is lost.

Crab pots are thick in this area off Tilghman. Robbie explains that men paint the floats different colors so they don't get their pots mixed up with someone else's. "We even have trouble with our own sometimes," he says. "If we hit a hot spot for crabs, we'll run a lot of pots. To

keep from pullin' the same line twice, we'll wrap a little piece of col-
ored duct tape on the floats on one line so we know we pulled that line
and not another. Sometimes the pots are so thick in a hot area you
can't even sail through 'em and it can get confusin', you know."

A captain calls on the radio to tell Robbie "This is a hell of a hobby,
ain't it?"

"If it keeps up like this Gary says we'll be losin' our trucks, houses, or
car," Robbie replies.

"Yea," says the captain on the other end. "The repo man will come
lookin' for us."

"Well, you know the bridgetender has his orders. If the repo man
comes onto the Island to get a truck, our boy will jack the bridge up so
he can't get on or off. He'll just jack her up is all." They both laugh and
work continues.

At 11:05 a.m. there is another sandwich break. Robbie calls Gary
on the LUCKY LADY to see if he's going in early and if he would take
our peeler crabs in to Miss Brenda. Gary says he's on his way in now
and will swing by the BRENDA II and pick them up. At 11:12 a.m.
Robbie is off his chair—this one was a seven-minute break.

Brian, 19, is looking tired. He has been living on the boat for a week
since starting work with Robbie. He is from the suburban town of
Woodbridge, Virginia, and after spending a year in college, wanted to
work with Chesapeake Bay watermen. "I looked at a map and thought
this would be a good crabbing area so I came down. I went to the local
store and asked around. I was real lucky to get this job and I hope I can
stick with it through the fall," he said.

Robbie says, "He's a real good boy but he's never been on the water.
I'm not sure how he'll hold up. If the crabs start runnin' and the sea
nettles get thick in the pots, I'll work him so hard he'll probably go
back to college and become a doctor rather than think about doing
this for a living!"

At 2:45 p.m., with 4½ bushels of males and a bushel of females on
board, all the pots have been pulled and rebaited. The men have not
been overly jovial today and neither have the conversations on the
radio. They are optimistic August will pick up and then there will be
money to be made. Robbie describes the mood perfectly, "I guess
things are more funnier when you do gooder!"

It's only 3:00 p.m. and Robbie wants to pull about 50 pots and store them on the roof of the BRENDA II for transport to the western shore tomorrow morning. He will add his new short line of pots to the ones already over there in the hope that crabs will move up the western shore. "They ain't movin' north of Smith Island, you know."

As Robbie pulls the pots, William dumps the bait out. Robbie then wraps the float line around the float and stores it inside the pot. William puts each pot on the engine box amidship and I pass them through a trap door in the roof to Brian who will stack and tie them down. It's 96° out there so Brian, being new at this "hobby" is feeling the end of the 12-hour day. He is moving slower and remains quiet.

Once the pots have been stored up top, Robbie asks me to take the helm while he, William, and Brian clean up. The area around and under the crab box is a mess with sea nettles that feel and look like soft jello, mud, water, toadfish, and crab claws. The men will scrub the boat down and clean up for tomorrow's departure at 4:00 a.m. As I maneuver the BRENDA II up the Tilghman coast, Robbie wants me to count the number of pots left in the line where we removed the 50. He needs to keep track of the number he is leaving behind on this particular set. As we reach the channel marker signaling the entrance to Knapps Narrows, I tell him there are 33 pots still in the water on that line.

Once in the Narrows, Robbie takes the helm and we tie up at a bulkhead where we unload the crabs for his buyer and receive 18 bushel baskets. These baskets will be stored with the 30 or so already on board. Such optimism.

We arrive back at the boat slip about 4:30 p.m. I get off the boat with James to talk to Brenda about her soft crab/peeler operation. William prepares to go home, Brian wants to take a shower, and Robbie starts filling the boat with fuel. We ended the day with about half the crabs needed to make a decent day's wages.

Soft Shells

Aside from the "hard" crab market, there is large market for "soft-shell" crabs. After molting from an old shell, the crab is very soft and weak. Within hours the crab's new shell begins to harden. It is only during the short period following molting that the "soft-shell" crab exists. Soft crabs must measure 3½ inches from one tip of their shell to the other in order to be legal size to sell.

The first commercial production of soft-shell crabs began in the 1850's in Crisfield, Maryland. Over the years, soft-shell crab producers learned to identify peelers—crabs ready to molt—and to isolate them in floating boxes, called crab floats or live boxes.

In the 1950's, producers developed a shore-based, flow-through float or tank system. About 58 percent of soft-shell producers currently use this system, which not only provides some protection for the peelers but less arduous work for the producers, as well.

In the 1970's, special shore-based traps specifically designed to attract and capture peelers were popularized. The "peeler pound" harvesting method took advantage of the crab's instinct to move to shallow water as molting approaches. Despite these advancements in harvesting methods, the majority of peelers were still captured "incidentally" during the hunt for hard crabs.

Harvesting soft-shell crabs still requires long hours of hard work. While soft-shell crabs might bring over $1 apiece, soft-shell production literally requires working 24-hours-a-day during shedding season. Brenda Wilson says it's worse than "minding a newborn baby." As she stands beside her 14 soft crab or peeler floats, each measuring about five feet by eight feet with water circulating constantly she says, "I come down here every four hours at night and every two hours during the day, 24 hours a day, seven days a week, all summer long. If they shed on you and you don't get them in that few hours, their shell will start to get hard. Soft crabs are bringing $20 a dozen for "whalers" or large, $16 a dozen for prime. She and her friend Pat walk around the huge wooden containers moving crabs from one float to another or removing ones that are soft. Even though William and Brian separated the peelers for her on board the BRENDA II, she and Pat will double-check each crab again. She explains that crabs with the pink or red lines on their flipper fins can be mixed male and female because they will shed at any time. They are the ones the women watch every couple of hours. The "green" flipper-finned peelers cannot be mixed with the "pink" or "red" because they will take longer to shed and will eat the others when they become soft. By July, Robbie says Brenda starts looking "like a Zombie."

She lets me and James test our eyes and tell her into which float to put which peelers. We were right about half the time!

From her little shed next to the floats and dock, she sells soft crabs to area restaurants, residents, and tourists. Bill Cummings' wife Jeane has a similar float operation across the Narrows about 100 feet away.

"If the men don't bring in the hard crabs we can make some money workin' our floats," Brenda says. And Robbie concurs saying, "The only real money I'm makin' is in peelers, but hell, that's Brenda's business, you know!"

Trotlining

Crossing the Kent Narrows Bridge from Kent Island at 2:20 a.m. on June 22, I begin to fascinate that truck drivers must never sleep. It seems whenever I leave this early in the morning to go out on a boat, the truckers are there on the highway. By 3:00 a.m. I am well down the Eastern Shore of the Chesapeake and there are more pick-ups on the road, more headlights visible in small marinas along the way, and activities pick up considerably as the clock approaches 4:00 a.m.

I will be going out trotlining for crabs with C.R. Wilson, who will be going into the ninth grade in September, and his "crew" Chris who's going into tenth grade and Brian Lowry who is in the sixth grade. As I wait in the parking lot besides C.R.'s boat TUFF e 'NUFF, I spot a boy on a bicycle racing across the Tilghman drawbridge, around the curve and into the parking lot. Chris has arrived. He says "hi" and that C.R. should be here any minute. Brenda Wilson drove him to get Brian and "when they get back we'll be underway."

Within ten minutes there is a beehive of activity on the dock. C.R. and Brian have arrived. Brenda has turned the lights on and is checking her peeler crabs which move constantly in their wooden floats. Robbie, Brian, and William of the BRENDA II are unloading clam bait for a day of crab potting, men down the line of boats are similarly busy. Four workboats are passing through the drawbridge to their crabbing grounds. While there is little conversation, VHF radios are on and captains are beginning to break the silence.

After he starts the engine, C.R. notes that the bilge pump is not working and asks Chris and Brian to look for pliers and a flashlight.

They can't find either and William, hearing the discussion, walks over from the BRENDA II and climbs aboard TUFF e 'NUFF.

"You goin' with me too!" C.R. exclaims.

"Hell, no," William says. "I ain't goin' out on no small boat!"

"Why, 'case it sinks?" Chris intercedes.

"Yea, I want to be on a big boat so I can run from side to side and all around the deck case I need time to plan out what I'm goin' to do if she goes down!" William exclaims with a chuckle. He leaves to go back and help Robbie.

C.R. borrows a flashlight and pliers from Robbie and, after finding a bad wire on the bilge switch decides we should leave anyway. "We'll just jiggle the wire every so often and she'll be all right," he says.

As we head out of the Narrows toward the Choptank River, C.R. explains that success in trotlining is dependent on two primary factors: the flow of the tide and where you lay your line. Crabs run with the tide so if there is a good tide they will bite, and if there is no tide they will "drop off."

"They'll jump off the bait in clear water too 'cause they can see the boat comin' for 'em. That's why we look for thunderstorms to cloud up the water a little," he says. "They really don't care much about the weather, it's mainly in the tides. Like yesterday, it was so rough the bow went under with every sea. It was hard on us but not on them crabs."

TUFF e 'NUFF has a plywood roof canopy like most of the other boats to provide protection from the sun and weather. The canopy runs two-thirds the length of the deck. She has a winder wheel attached to the side which C.R. uses to reel in the long trotline at the end of the day. There is a two-foot by four-foot wooden box, similar to the one on the other crabbing boats, that will be used for culling, (sorting) the crabs we catch into baskets for males, females, and peelers. On the aft of the boat to starboard, hanging out over the water a couple of feet, is a foot-long stainless steel roller that looks like a rolling pin. There are two crab nets and a boat hook hanging parallel to the roof in two rope loops. The trotline itself is a mile long with small string loops every six feet. The loops hold a small three-inch piece of salted eel by way of a slip knot. The line is stored in two sections in 55-gallon trash cans. There are two other plastic cans on board, one that holds eels for bait and one for salt.

An orange buoy marks the spot where we will begin running our line. Connected to the buoy is a pipe anchor and a lead line of rope, then a length of heavy chain. The chain holds the trotline to the bottom which is where the crabs will feed on the eel. Once we are in place and C.R. has attached the trotline to the line coming off the chain, he asks Chris to get ready. As TUFF e 'NUFF takes off slowly, Chris throws in the pipe anchor, buoy line with chain, and then the trotline begins to leave the trash cans. The eel was put on the day before and salted down for the night. Once we have the 5,280 feet of line out, C.R. wraps the end of the trotline around a cleat and uses the boat to pull out any slack. He then instructs Chris to toss in the second buoy and pipe anchor. The trotline has been set and we head back up the line to where we started. This gives the bait a chance to set and the crabs a few minutes to begin breakfast.

Minutes later as we approach the starting buoy, C.R. takes the boat hook, reaches into the water and lifts the trotline over the small roller attached to the side of the boat. He then leans against the side, and holding a crab net in his right hand and the steering stick is his left hand, sets the throttle for a slow movement forward. We travel parallel to the trotline and the movement raises it up from the bottom, breaking the surface inches from the roller. This is where the feeding crabs appear and C.R. can scoop them with the net and fling them into the culling box. Once at the other end of the line, we'll turn around and do it again, and again, and again.

It is interesting to watch these three boys operate. They are very responsible and perform their set-up activities with care. They also, however, take any lull in activity as an opportunity to "horse" around and punch at each other, especially Chris and Brian. C.R. is at the controls so his physical fooling around is limited—his verbal is not. And they jest, play, and talk continuously as they work.

As C.R. watches the line break the surface, he is frustrated with the choppy water. It makes it difficult to keep the boat in the right position while moving up the line and he has missed two large male crabs. Chris ignores C.R.'s problem, he is engaged in tutoring Brian on a new way to tell the mature male crabs. "They have hair under their armpits. Go ahead and look under that flipper," he explains seriously to the sixth grader, trying not to laugh.

C.R. cuts into the activity by asking Chris to cull and Brian to start cutting up bait which will be used at the end of the day. Chris says "good" because he doesn't care to handle the slimy eels or to cut them into strips. Without a word, Brian puts a cutting board on the engine box and reaches into the plastic barrel, grabs a handful of eels and starts to cut them. He throws the head and tail-end overboard and puts the saved strips in a small tin bucket for later use. As Brian cuts, C.R. explains that he will buy about $120 of eel a week. He says that "a girl on one of these boats can bait a coil of line (600 feet) in the fastest time yet—7.7 minutes. Tyin' a piece of eel on every six feet. It takes me twice that time. She's right fast," he says.

As the trotlining continues, we are getting large crabs but very few small peelers or females. This is consistent with what the crab potters are doing. The crabs are slow and C.R. says he would like to get five bushels today but will probably only get two or three. "It's all we're gettin'," he says. "My Uncle Charlie over there has his line working an edge (where the bottom drops off to deeper water) and he's haulin' in six or seven bushels. That's more than anybody else around here. But I'll tell you the biggest crabs goin' is on the Miles River. Thirty-one crabs to a bushel (the average is about 50). When the line comes up it looks like you're pullin' in an anchor! That's how big they are," he says as he turns to Chris to complain that after two hours and 15 minutes we only have one bushel, worth $55.

At 7:30 a.m. C.R. notices for the third time this morning that the bilge is not pumping water from the boat and it is building up below deck. It must not only be the bad switch wire causing the problem so he instructs Chris to take a screwdriver and see if the drain hole in the side of the boat is clogged. Chris sticks the instrument in but no water comes out. C.R. tells him to lift the floor boards so he can unclamp the hose leading from the bilge pump to the drain hole to see if that hose is clogged. Once the hose is free we notice the pump itself isn't working. As Chris proceeds with an inspection, C.R. is continuing to move down the trotline. He is putting crabs in a bushel basket—the culling box had to be moved to free the floor boards over the bilge. Brian continues to sort crabs as Chris reveals a clogged bilge pump motor. Once it is cleaned and reassembled it drains the boat quickly of excess water. C.R. and his crew are thrilled.

With the bilge problem corrected, C.R. decides to take a look at the engine shaft. He senses a problem and asks us to remove the engine box and rear floor boards. As we move the boards forward he wants a large wrench to tighten a shaft bolt. "Hand me that wrench, Brian," he instructs. Reaching down, neither he nor Chris can manage to get a lock on the bolt nor tighten it after several attempts. I sense he is right about the problem but lacking the skill to solve it completely. The episode ends with the "Captain" saying "Never mind. Put the boards and box cover back. My father will fix it later for me." Case closed. I am impressed with how he took charge and thought so clearly in analyzing each situation, and, the other teenagers responded without hesitation to their "Captain's" requests and the boat's needs.

"If we go in by 1:30 p.m. I'll get her straight today. I need to put new points and plugs in her and check the wiring for the bilge," C.R. says.

Every hour or so the boys begin fooling around with each other. Chris jumps overboard to cool off from the 98° heat. I notice that C.R. is cautious that the other 12 crabbing boats working in this area don't see this recreational activity. He seems to want to have a good time but not let other captains know how good a time can be had aboard TUFF e 'NUFF.

After noon, the crabs are slacking off and we have four bushels of hard crabs and three peelers. C.R. decides to take up the trotline and head in. He pulls the boat up against the buoy and hooks the submerged line with the boat hook. Chris grabs the line and pulls in the buoy and pipe anchor as well as the line with the "anchor" chain. Once the chain is on board C.R. wraps the end of the trotline in the winder. With the boat moving forward ever so slowly, the winder begins reeling in the line very quickly and depositing it in a pile on deck. When about 1,200 feet of line is on board C.R. asks Chris to get the eel he and Brian chopped earlier and begin baiting the line for the next day. Brian watches the rest of the line coming into the boat to make sure it doesn't get tangled.

Baiting, it seems, is a "science" like everything else these men do. Standing over a 55-gallon trash can, Chris grabs one end of the trotline and begins feeding it into the can. As he comes across a bait noose he will remove the existing bait and put on a new piece. He will do this every six feet for the 1,200 plus feet of line he has in his pile. Brian will do a pile and C.R. will do a pile to total the 5,280 feet of line needing bait. As the boys fill the cans they will periodically spread salt on the eel and line to preserve it until it's used. There is competition between them on speed and complaints about who has the longest line to bait. C.R. has assured that he is the fastest and will do more line. Brian will simply remove old bait from one coil (600 feet) and store the line in a bushel basket. C.R. doesn't want to use it for a few days.

Suddenly, as the boys are working on the lines, a bushel basket of crabs slides overboard and bobbles up and down. We all run to the side and I try to snag it with a boat hook. When this proves unsuccessful and the prospects of losing the $55 bushel to the bottom seems more and more real, C.R. tells Chris to "go overboard and grab her before she goes under." Chris immediately dives overboard and clutches the basket. When we circle to pick him up, I lift the crabs out and then grab him by the seat of the pants and help him over the side. There is no overboard ladder on the boat.

Re-baiting continues and is completed in little over an hour. On the way into the harbor Chris and Brian begin to clean up and scrub the boat down. C.R. pulls alongside the crab boat BIG DADDY and goes aboard to visit with his grandfather for a few minutes. According to Brian, C.R. performs this ritual just about every day they go out. We all wait patiently for him to return.

Back in the Narrows we get gas, ice, and sodas for tomorrow's trip, sell the crabs, and watch and listen as C.R. socializes with many boats and men. He tells all about his bilge and carburetor problems. The buyer at Harrison's packing house says, "Tell your father to look at the carburetor, C.R. And listen, make sure you take care of your crabs. Feel how hot this basket cover is. Well, you left it in the sun—keep 'em in the shade under your canopy. It's too damn hot to leave 'em out." C.R. concurs with the criticism and recommendation.

"And listen, a couple of these baskets are a little light of a full bushel," the buyer says.

"No, they ain't," C.R. emphasizes, "they just settled in. They was full weren't they, Chris?"

"Okay, we'll pay you for all of 'em. But be mindful next time and consider it your birthday present!" he says.

The buyer is smart to let the young boy know what he expects and rewarding him for his efforts at the same time. I am sure C.R. got the message and will employ its wisdom next time he sells crabs. As we pull away from the packing house and C.R. continues to talk to every captain he sees, one of them looks at me, chuckles, and says, "If he ain't the damndest thing on these waters." I think he's right. I leave an hour later as C.R. heads off on his bicycle to swim in the pool and be a kid again.

As I leave the Eastern Shore, crossing the Bay Bridge I think about my day trotlining with C.R., Brian, and Chris. Young watermen—will they still work on the water when they are older?

My year with them has about finished and most of the harvests have been discussed. There is so much about the watermen and their life-styles that I didn't cover or tell about, so many stones left unturned and roads not traveled. Nevertheless, the next time I see the men, women, and children of the water it will not be as a researcher or writer, but as an advocate and friend.

Conclusion

As I contemplate the watermen's activities over the past year, several thoughts have remained in my mind consistently throughout this project:

I have developed a deep appreciation for the watermen and women—their lifestyles, work ethics, respect for nature, value sys-tems, perseverance and openness. I have found that I love being with them and around them. They are human encyclopedias on the Bay and her inhabitants and I am honored to have had the opportunity to learn from them. They make me want to carry their "cross." And as melodramatic as it sounds, I would be less than honest if I said it were not true.

I am sad, in a way, for having reached the "end of the harvest." James and I will now go on to other projects and leading our normal lives. The watermen will also go on and they will continue to do what they have done for generations: work the water. I know many will not com-promise and work off the water or accept government assistance, for their faith will remain in the fate that the Chesapeake will deliver.

There are many challenges facing the Chesapeake and its men and women. All of us, watermen and concerned individuals alike must work

- To restore the fisheries
- To curb the flow of nutrients—especially phosphorus and nitrogen—the "fertilizers" that fuel the growth of algae which depletes oxygen and kills underwater grasses
- To stop the flow of deadly toxicants into the Bay ecosystem
- To develop sound scientific, management, and use policies to assure the restoration of the nation's most productive estuary.

When you enter the open waters of the Chesapeake Bay or the solitude of one of her creeks or rivers, it is easy to fall into the romantic euphoria created by the entire scenario. This is even easier to do when a skipjack or crabbing skiff passes by has its silhouette carved on the horizon. But *Sunup to Sundown* was not written to conjure up romantic notions about life on the water. Rather it was prepared to represent the reality of that lifestyle. A rugged life of dedication, with an appreciation of the beauty and grace of the Chesapeake, but not consumed by its wonder.

It is my hope that all citizens will grow to understand the issues surrounding the survival of the bay and how they can play a part in meeting the challenges they present. In the meantime, the watermen remain at the mercy of mother nature and Uncle Sam—they have little power against either. *Sunup to Sundown* should help you understand this very significant American sub-culture. And, as Dr. Rita Caldwell said, maybe we should start listening to the watermen.

We will leave in pitch black silence
        you and I
to cross the Bay
while others
        linger in the pleasures
        of their own dream worlds

We will wait in numbing apprehension
        you and I
to face gale and ice
while others
        lie in the warmth
        of their own circumstances

We will see through the night
        you and I
into a new sunrise
while others
        expect the immortal light
        to arrive much before they do.

"As we leave in the pitch of the night, I gaze skyward and wonder about the eyes of ancestors hidden behind the stars. Are they watching us heading for open water and, perhaps, wishing us well."

MSB

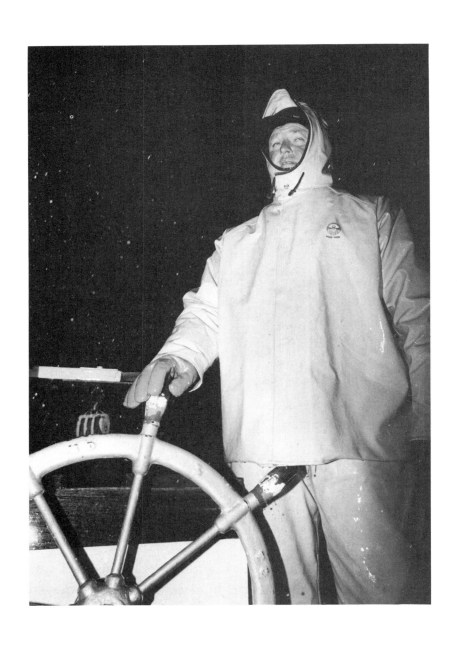